IT MUST HAVE BEEN AN ANGEL

Marjorie Lewis Lloyd

Pacific Press Publishing Association
Boise, Idaho
Oshawa, Ontario, Canada

Cover by Adán Saldaña

Library of Congress Cataloging in Publication Data
Lloyd, Marjorie Lewis
  It must have been an angel.

  (A Redwood paperback; 119)
  Includes bibliographical references.
  1. Angels. I. Title.
BT966.2.L55   235'.3   79-23418

ISBN 0-8163-0363-0

89 90 91 92 93 ● 5 4

Contents

Dedication

To my angel—who must have been
chosen for his patience—
I dedicate this book

It Must Have Been
an Angel

The corner of Broadway and Forty-second Street in New York City is one of the busiest in the world. But one day a cat threaded her way along the sidewalk and came up to the curb. She was holding a baby kitten in her mouth by the back of the neck, as cats do. She wanted to cross the street, but she was confused and frightened by the roar of trucks and buses and cabs. Several times she stepped cautiously off the curb and then came back. It was just too dangerous.

And then something happened. The traffic officer saw her. Immediately he put up his hands and stopped the traffic both ways, because of course he couldn't know which way she wanted to go.

Now when a traffic officer lifts his hand, it isn't a request. There's power behind it. Instantly all traffic stood still. The cat saw her chance and darted across with her little one to safety. And then the rush and the roar resumed.

The cat never knew that she was the object of special care. She never knew that a hand had been lifted especially for her—and that back of that hand was all the authority of the city of New York.

We, too, never know how often a hand is lifted for us—with all the authority of Heaven back of it. We are reluctant to think that God could be interested, even aware, of the needs of a single individual—especially of one on a tiny, seemingly insignificant planet such as ours. We hesitate to speak of angel hands being lifted in our behalf—even if we *have* been told that we are worth more than sparrows. We speak of coincidence and good fortune. And some of us even call it luck.

Yet down through the centuries angels have walked beside the children of men—comforting, guiding, encouraging, delivering from danger. Most of the time they have stayed in the shadows, only occasionally darting across our field of vision, dazzling us with their brightness, bringing us some message from the throne. But in all times and in all lands, including our own, they have left the indelible marks of their presence and their care. And we interrupt our wonder to exclaim, with conviction if not with proof, "It must have been an angel!"

The story of the magnificent ministry of angels, those patient celestial beings assigned to us on planet Earth, has never been fully told. Nor will it ever be. But we can begin!

It was a sleepy, snowy day in a winter that had already been far too long. It was 1964. And it was Friday.

The snow that had been falling for two days finally did let up, and Lowell Thomas, Jr., left for the airport. As an Alaska state senator, he had business in Fairbanks.

His wife, Tay, and the children—Anne, eight, and David, six—waved good-bye and closed the door quickly because it was still below freezing outside. At about five o'clock, because Anne had a headache, they went upstairs to rest and watch TV, and they took off their shoes so they could sit on the beds.

About a half hour later Tay heard a rumbling sound. She had often heard guns firing at a nearby Army base. But this was not the rumbling of guns!

She shouted "Earthquake!" and jumped off the bed, grabbing Anne and calling to David across the hall. They had reached the front door when the house began to shake. And as they ran out into the snow, David was crying "Mommy, I'm in bare feet!"

The earth was jolting back and forth with unbelievable force, and they were flung violently to the ground. The hallway they had just run through split in two. They heard the sounds of crashing glass and splintering wood. A tree crashed to the ground. Their garage collapsed.

Tay Thomas describes what happened. She says the earth began breaking up and buckling all about them. Suddenly between her and Anne a great crack opened in the snow. She stared in disbelief as the trench widened, apparently bottomless, separating her from her child. She grabbed the hand Anne reached out to her and was able to pull her across the chasm.

They were left, she says, on a wildly bucking slab of earth. Suddenly it tilted sharply, and they had to hang on to keep from slipping into a yawning crevasse. The earth seemed to be rising just ahead of them. She had the weird feeling that they were riding backward on a monstrous Ferris wheel, going down, down toward the water. Their house had stood on a high bluff overlooking Cook Inlet. But now the entire face of the bluff had fallen to sea level. A few feet away, at the water's edge, lay the roof of their house.

I'm using her words to describe it. She says all she could think of was that the water would rise as earth tumbled into it and they would be trapped. The cliffs above them were sheer, with great sections of sand and clay still falling. They had to find a way up that cliff, but the children were too frightened to walk. They kept crying, "We'll die! We'll die!"

In that desperate situation she looked up at the sky and silently cried out, "Jesus, where are You? I thought You'd be with us at the end!" And suddenly she felt a tremendous peace. She knew that He *was* with her—not up in the sky somewhere, but right beside her.

At that moment a man appeared above them. They called for help, and he shouted that he would look for a rope. Then six or eight men appeared at the top of the cliff. One of them, a stranger, climbed down. The children threw their arms around him. He took off his black wool jacket, put it around Anne, boosted David into his arms, and led them all back up along the rope.

At the top of the cliff Tay Thomas turned to thank their rescuer. He had disappeared. They were never able to learn his identity. Had God sent an angel in answer to a trusting prayer? Was eight-year-old Anne wearing a jacket that belonged to an angel?[1]

We cannot know for sure. But there's a familiar pattern here. And of one thing we can be certain. It's the sort of kindness angels like to do!

From a pen dipped in inspiration we read: "Not until the providences of God are seen in the light of eternity shall we understand what we owe to the care and interposition of His angels."[2]

But we worship a God who doesn't want to wait. He shares a few of His secrets now!

Now You See Them

Pastor Merritt Warren had not been in China long when he made this particular trip. Like most every journey he would take in that country, it was full of danger, leading through a robber-infested area.

He had been traveling several days when he was delayed one afternoon by a stranger who invited him to his home. He had learned that Pastor Warren was a Seventh-day Adventist minister and wanted to ask questions about his belief. Pastor Warren, of course, was glad for the opportunity to talk with one who showed such interest.

He thought he had plenty of time. The coolies, with the boxes, had gone on. The village of Chintaipu was only five miles away. He could easily ride that distance before dark. As he was leaving, however, his host told him that it was nearly three times that far. He warned him that it was not safe to travel in that region after dark.

Hastily he mounted his horse and hurried over the low hills. Just at dark he reached a small village along the way. He hoped the carriers would be waiting there. But he learned that they had gone on up the mountain.

What could he do? The carriers had his food and his bedding. And he must pay for their lodging wherever they stopped. He knew now that he was in danger.

The coolies had his lantern too, and he would have to have a lantern. So he bought a Chinese paper lantern, and the shopkeeper lighted it for him.

But in a little while, as he walked ahead, leading his horse down the slippery stones of the mountain, the candle sputtered and went out. He started to light another, but then he said to himself, "Now, look here! You can see better with the lantern, but so can the robbers. If they are following you, the light will help them more than it will help you." So he trudged on, hoping the robbers wouldn't hear the clank of the horse's shoes on the stone steps.

At the bottom of the mountain he came to a bridge made of stone slabs. He couldn't see what he was crossing—it might be a stream or a chasm. He could see only the dim trail and the bridge. Beyond the bridge the trail turned to the right and began another ascent.

About a hundred and fifty feet from the bridge, to his right, Pastor Warren saw a house and a light burning inside. The house was about fifty feet long and seemed to front on the road. A door in the center opened as he arrived, and two men came out.

Pastor Warren had a good excuse for stopping, for he was alone and without a light. Speaking in the humble manner used by the Chinese, he said politely, "May your younger brother borrow a light from his older brother?"

"I shall be glad to give my brother a light," one of the men answered. He stepped inside and returned with a piece of flaming bamboo. When the candle in the lantern had been lighted, one of the men asked, "Where are you going?"

"To Chintaipu."

"I am traveling that way myself."

"I shall be honored to have my older brother lead me," Pastor Warren answered.

They started off together, talking as they traveled. Merritt asked questions, but he was careful not to say anything that would sound as if he were trying to identify him. If the man were a robber, the situation would be dangerous.

Finally the man said, "There are many robbers through this section, and they are robbing all the time. No one is really safe on this road. I am glad I could come along with you."

That was strange. The man wore ordinary clothes, the rice-straw sandals of the common peasant. Why would a robber try to rob him? And why was this stranger happy to have a foreigner with him?

Soon they came to a place where a path branched off. The Chinese said, "I must leave you here."

"Aren't you going to Chintaipu?"

"No, I'm turning off here."

"How much farther is it to Chintaipu?"

"Not very far. You will be there right away. I am glad I could walk with you."

When Merritt arrived in the village, he found the people worried about his safety. They told of many travelers who had been robbed. And some had been killed. The young missionary had reason to be thankful—very, very thankful!

The next time he traveled that way, he was anxious to see by daylight the places where he had walked that dark night. It was all just as he remembered it. The shop where he had bought the lantern. The climb up the mountain. The stone steps down the other side. The ravine with the stone slabs for crossing. As he started up the slope, he looked for the house. *No house was there!*

Had the house burned down? "It has to be here! It

was a large house, and it stood right here!"

But as he examined that slope, he saw that the ground had never been leveled at any place along the road. It would have been impossible to build a house without leveling a large piece of ground. But there was no level ground. The hillside had never been disturbed!

No wonder he stood silently with bowed head. He knew now that an angel had walked with him that dark night![1]

Says an inspired writer, "We need to understand better than we do the mission of the angels. It would be well to remember that every true child of God has the co-operation of heavenly beings. Invisible armies of light and power attend the meek and lowly ones who believe and claim the promises of God."[2]

And from the same pen we read: "Not until the providences of God are seen in the light of eternity shall we understand what we owe to the care and interposition of His angels. Celestial beings have taken an active part in the affairs of men. They have appeared in garments that shone as the lightning; they have come as men, in the garb of wayfarers. They have accepted the hospitalities of human homes; they have acted as guides to benighted travelers."[3]

Angels as guides? Yes, again and again!

Charlotte, many years ago, was a student at Pacific Union College. At the insistence of the dean of women, she had memorized the words, "The angel of the Lord encampeth round about them that fear him, and delivereth them." Psalm 34:7. But little did she realize how soon she would need the assurance of those words.

To help with expenses Charlotte traveled twice a week by bus some distance from the campus to a town where she worked for a fine family who paid her generously. All went well until one night, tired and not watching carefully, she boarded the wrong bus—one bound for San Francisco.

There she was in the big city, alone and surrounded by strangers. She had no idea, in that huge terminal, how to find a bus that would take her back the way she had come. There was not a single woman on the loading platform. A drunk was trying to make conversation. The information booth was closed for the night. Not a policeman was in sight. And bus drivers were too busy even to hear her timid question. What should she do? She was frightened and confused.

Then, like a flash, she remembered the words she had memorized—the words the dean had told her she would need someday. "The angel of the Lord encampeth round about them that fear him, and delivereth them."

Finding a rest room, she went in and locked the door. Then she fell to her knees and prayed, "Dear Lord, I'm tired and lost. I'm afraid. I don't know anyone here. Please help me find my way home. According to Thy Word, deliver me. Amen."

Then she stepped out into the main area of the terminal again. Just at that moment a young man passed in front of her, and she noticed immediately that he was carrying what appeared to be a large black Bible!

A Bible! Could it be that he was a student returning to P.U.C.? At least he must be a good man—a man with a Bible. She followed him. He led her along several long corridors to another part of the terminal and finally up a flight of stairs to a remote loading platform. She never could have found her way. And there it was, a bus ready to pull out, with big letters on the front—ANGWIN.

Now right at this point it is necessary either to

discard the story as false or accept it as a miracle. For anyone at all familiar with Pacific Union College knows that no bus, unless it were a chartered bus, would ever pull out of the San Francisco terminal with "Angwin" on the front. It would likely be necessary to change buses in Vallejo. Or even if a bus should go directly to St. Helena, it would not be negotiating the tight curves up the hill to Angwin. So the story becomes "incredible"—which, according to the *Random House Dictionary*, means "so extraordinary as to seem impossible." Yet should we limit God—or question the ability of an angel to write six letters on the front of a bus, even if it was not going all the way to that destination?

But back to Charlotte. She followed the young man with the Bible onto the bus. There was only one seat left. But the young man stopped, as if to speak to the driver, and let her pass. She took the seat, amazed and thankful, and continued to stare at the young man, whose back was turned.

And then something strange happened. The bus driver didn't seem to see the young man at all. He turned and got off the bus, but no one paid any attention. Only Charlotte continued to watch him intently. She followed his form a few feet, in her steady vision. And then, with her eyes fixed upon him, he simply vanished—like a light going out![4]

Was he an angel—guiding a tired, lost girl? You decide.

A mother and daughter, with two Saint Bernards, were traveling through Arkansas when a news bulletin came over the radio: "Due to the extensive flooding in southern Tennessee and Missouri, the bridge in Crithersville, Missouri, has been washed out. We suggest you take the Brown's Ferry crossing instead."

But where was Brown's Ferry? A gas station attendant gave them directions, and they drove off into the approaching darkness. Were the directions accurate? And were they following them correctly? Again and again they had reason to wonder. In the wind and the rain and the mud they seemed to be driving straight into the isolation of nowhere.

Debbie was crying. What if they were lost? Even the Saint Bernards seemed to know that something was wrong. "Deb," said mother, "I'm not very religious, but maybe we ought to pray. At least we'll be ready if something does happen."

"OK," replied Debbie. "You pray."

"I can't. I'm driving. Do you want to go off the levee?"

The car slowed as Debbie prayed, and somehow they felt better. And there was one other consolation. Volkswagens were supposed to float for half an hour.

Finally they came to a place where the road ahead was flooded. Mother stepped out of the car to see how deep the water was. She could see a strong current on ahead. She had gone about forty feet, turned back, and was almost to the car when another set of head-lights appeared from nowhere. The car stopped. There seemed to be a man inside. "We're trying to get to Brown's Ferry," she told him.

"Well," he drawled, with a long pause, "I can get you all across this flooded area here, and the ferry is just up the road a piece." And he added, "You be sure and follow closely now."

And of course she did. Slowly and cautiously she followed the cream-colored car, with the current tugging demandingly. Once across the troubled waters, she pulled up beside the man. "Thank you so much," she said gratefully.

"That's quite all right. Just keep on going 'bout two or three more miles, and you'll come to the ferry."

Thanking him again, she pulled away slowly. But looking into the rearview mirror she could see no headlights, no car, no houses, nothing. "Look back there! There's no one there!" she nearly shouted at Debbie.

Debbie looked back into the blackness. "You're right!"[5]

"They have acted as guides to benighted travelers." Remember?

Isaac Neabaugo has reason to remember. In his own words he tells what happened as he was trying to introduce Jesus to the people of his own village in the highlands of New Guinea:

"One day I left place where I stay and go to another place to visit people. When I was there visiting people, the rain came and flood came and I have no way to across the floody river and I kneel down just bank of the river and ask the Lord to make my way. When I opened my eyes the man was stand beside me and said, 'Where you want to go?'

"The man said, 'If you want to go to the other side of the river you just follow me.' I follow and man take me to other side of the river and we stand together and I turn my face away from the man and when I turn back I didn't see him anymore.

"That what the Lord had done to me."[6]

Says a writer whose words can be trusted, "The Bible shows us God in His high and holy place, not in a state of inactivity, not in silence and solitude, but surrounded by ten thousand times ten thousand and thousands of thousands of holy beings, all waiting to do His will. Through these messengers He is in active communication with every part of His dominion. By His Spirit He is everywhere present. Through the agency of His Spirit and His angels, He ministers to the children of men.

"Above the distractions of the earth He sits enthroned; all things are open to His divine survey; and from His great and calm eternity He orders that which His providence sees best."[7]

Angels. Assigned to us on planet Earth. Sometimes we see them. Most of the time we don't. But never are we beyond the reach of their untiring care!

Now You Don't

Hazel Jackson believes in angels.

She and her husband were returning from a vacation in Death Valley. They had just reached the top of a mountain when her husband discovered that they had no brakes. Their hearts seemed to stop.

They were driving a heavy car and pulling a travel trailer, and already they were gaining speed down the mountain. On one side was an abrupt drop lined with huge boulders all the way to the bottom. On the other side it was straight up. No brakes. Accelerating speed. Death stalking them on either side. All they could do was pray.

Down, down the mountain, faster and faster they went, careening, it seemed, toward certain death. But suddenly, for no visible reason, the car skidded to a stop!

Her husband dashed out of the car and blocked the wheels with large rocks. And there on the mountain they thanked God for sparing their lives, and they marveled at how He had done it.

But they still had a problem—how to get down off the mountain with no brakes. Just then a service car from the station seven miles down in the valley pulled up alongside. The driver said he had received a call that someone on the mountain was in trouble. They told him they certainly were in trouble, but they had made no call. There was no phone anywhere around.

They waited while the driver checked the entire mountain, trying to discover who had called for help. He found no one else on the entire mountain and returned to assist the Jacksons.[1]

Who made that phone call? Who stopped the car in its wild ride? Do we have to see an angel to know that one is around?

"If you make the Most High your dwelling—even the Lord, who is my refuge—then no harm will befall you, no disaster will come near your tent. For he will command his angels concerning you to guard you in all your ways; they will lift you up in their hands, so that you will not strike your foot against a stone." Psalm 91:9-12, N.I.V.

But who are the angels? Are they the spirits of men and women who have died, as some believe? No. Angels were present when this world was created. And angels were assigned to guard the gate of the Garden of Eden as soon as Adam and Eve had sinned and been evicted from their garden home. How could they be the spirits of those who had died when no one had died yet?

It was David who said, "What is man, that thou are mindful of him? and the son of man, that thou visitest him? For thou hast made him a little lower than the angels, and hast crowned him with glory and honour." Psalm 8:4, 5.

A little lower than the angels. Evidently angels and men are separate and distinct. Created to inhabit heaven, they are a little higher order than man.

But angels, ever since man sinned and direct communication with the Creator was broken, have been given a very special assignment. "Are not all angels ministering spirits sent to serve those who will inherit salvation?" Hebrews 1:14, N.I.V.

Angels are commissioned to help and protect us. And Jesus indicated that an angel, a special angel, is assigned to each individual. For He said, "See that you do not look down on one of these little ones. For I tell you that their angels in heaven always see the face of my Father in heaven." Matthew 18:10, N.I.V.

Are angels simply doing their duty? Or are they genuinely interested in us? Evidently they are, for Jesus said, "There is . . . rejoicing in heaven over one sinner who repents." Luke 15:7, N.I.V.

Angels turn up repeatedly in the Bible record. An angel was sent to Daniel in the den of lions. An angel rescued Peter from prison. An angel prepared food for Elijah. An angel stayed the hand of Abraham when he was about to take the life of his son. Angels led Lot, his wife, and two daughters out of Sodom—just before the fire and brimstone.

But how much are the angels able to do for us? Are they really able to protect us? How much power do they have?

Let me answer it this way. On one occasion God's people were threatened by the Assyrian army. And God sent a single angel—just one angel—through the enemy camp one night. In the morning 185,000 soldiers were dead!

Evidently there is no lack of power. If angels are hindered in doing what they sincerely want to do for us, it is because they are restrained by God's wisdom—or by man's free choice. Angels cannot be expected to protect us from dangers that we deliberately choose.

But why, you wonder—why is it that angels so seldom make themselves visible to men? Why do they keep in the background? Why don't they come out in the open and let us see what they are doing for us?

I don't pretend to know the full answer. But we might find a clue in the experience of the apostle John on the island of Patmos as he was being given the book of Revelation. "At this I fell at his feet to worship him. But he said to me, 'Do not do it! . . . Worship God!' " Revelation 19:10, N.I.V.

And it happened again. 'I, John, am the one who heard and saw these things. And when I had heard and seen them, I fell down to worship at the feet of the angel who had been showing them to me. But he said to me, 'Do not do it! . . . Worship God!' " Revelation 22:8, 9, N.I.V.

Would we not be tempted, as John was tempted, to worship an angel who revealed his presence to us? Could this be one reason why angels so seldom make their presence known? Of one thing I am certain. Angels are anxious that the focus of attention should not be upon themselves but upon the Lord Jesus. They want to stay in the background. They want Christ to have the throne.

Even so, we can know that angels are with us. We can have their companionship. And we can know that we have their full support in every attempt to lift up Jesus before a fallen world.

Harry Schrillo, a dedicated layman who loved his Lord, also loved to sing His praise. I am told that he had a beautiful voice. And he used it for more than song. Let me share with you one little glimpse of his experience in working for his Lord.

He was studying the Bible with a fine young couple. They were sincere in their desire to learn. But they did not accept everything without question. They often brought up objections that must be met. On one particular evening the subject scheduled was one that Harry thought might be difficult for them to accept. He expressed his concern to his wife, Florence, and suggested that they pray about it. They went into the bedroom, knelt in prayer, and he left for his appointment.

That evening, to his surprise, everything he presented was accepted without question. The truth he presented from the Scriptures met with no resistance whatever. He never knew why it had been so different that evening, except that he and Florence had prayed especially about it.

It was several years later—after Harry died, I believe—that the wife in that home told Ruth Grunke, a friend of the Schrillos, what had happened. She said that when she went to the door to let Harry in, there was a halo of light about his head. And that halo of light remained through the entire study. His face seemed unusually happy and shining. Somehow everything seemed clear to them, and, with such an evidence of divine approval, how could they resist the truth that was presented?[2]

Florence Schrillo tells me that a similar light surrounded Harry once as he studied with another couple.

"All who engage in ministry are God's helping hand," we are told. "They are co-workers with the angels; rather, they are the human agencies through whom the angels accomplish their mission. Angels speak through their voices, and work by their hands. And the human workers, co-operating with heavenly agencies, have the benefit of their education and experience."[3]

In the future life, we read from the same pen, "every redeemed one will understand the ministry of angels in his own life. The angel who was his guardian from his earliest moment; the angel who watched his steps, and covered his head in the day of peril; the angel who

22

was with him in the valley of the shadow of death, who marked his resting place, who was the first to greet him in the resurrection morning—what will it be to hold converse with him, and to learn the history of divine interposition in the individual life, of heavenly co-operation in every work for humanity!"[4]

And those who, like Harry Schrillo, have walked and worked with angels unawares will see the result of their labor!

Alice Zarate was new in the literature ministry when it happened. Magazine workers in the Philippines usually make their calls two by two. But on this particular day it was necessary for her to work alone, and for that reason she prayed especially for both guidance and protection.

She was working in an area where the people were quite prejudiced against the type of work she was doing. As she approached a large house, she was met at the door by two large German police dogs, followed by their owner. The owner seemed surprised that the dogs were so silent and calm, and she invited Alice in.

So far the story is not unusual. But imagine, if you can, how Alice felt when the lady of the house placed two chairs instead of one, as if for two visitors! More than that, the lady addressed the second chair as if someone were sitting there. And Alice seemed to hear a quiet voice talking with the lady about the magazine!

Apparently whoever was in that second chair excused herself, and the lady accompanied her to the door. Then she remarked to Alice that her companion looked becoming in white. She asked about her religion, and Alice told her that she was a Seventh-day Adventist.

She wanted to tell her hostess that she really was working alone. But under the circumstances it just didn't seem appropriate.

The visitor in white must have returned, for the lady of the house now invited them both to stay for lunch. She set two places for her visitors. And when Alice stole a glance at the other place setting she saw that half of the glass of milk was gone, and half the slice of bread!

As Alice left the home, the owner placed a friendly hand on her shoulder, and it appeared that the other hand was placed on the shoulder of a person at her side.

Alice never did see her companion, but she remembered these words found in *Gospel Workers*, page 515: "Those who labor for the good of others are working in union with the heavenly angels. They have their constant companionship, their unceasing ministry."[5]

Guards in White

The latter half of the fifties. Those were troubled years for Indonesia. Terrorism was rampant. And Indonesia Union College, located near Bandung, Java, was in the center of it. In fact, the college was a prime target, for it had so many of the things terrorists wanted—stores of rice and other food, office machines, cameras, even hi-fi equipment. Teachers and students lived under the constant threat of attack. Homes and entire villages were being burned out. Yet for some reason the expected invasion of the campus never came. Garth Thompson, stationed there at that time as Bible teacher and pastor, told me the story.

One Sunday morning the villagers were very agitated. Two or three of their number, just the night before, had been captured by terrorists who demanded that they serve as guides for their destructive activities. And with guns at their heads, what could the villagers do but agree?

Where did they want to go? Down to the school. And the villagers panicked. "Not there!"

"Yes, that's exactly where we're going! And we'll shoot you if you don't cooperate!"

The captives were quaking with fear. And the terrorists asked, "Why? Why not the school?"

25

The villagers explained, "They have so many of those guards in white. We aren't going to tangle with them! We won't go anywhere near!"

And at the risk of their lives they disappeared into the bush!

Of course the Thompsons asked, when this was reported to them, "What do you mean—guards in white? We don't know anything about any guards."

But the villagers only responded, "Why, of course, we've all seen them!"

And evidently those guards in white kept a careful watch, for never once during those troubled years was an attack made on the college campus.[1]

It is not often that God's people are permitted to see their protectors. We do not need to see them. But again and again they have protected us by revealing their presence to the vision of our enemies. Guards in white. Shining watchmen. Soldiers. Uniformed guards. Men in white robes. Whatever they are called by those who see them, we can know that they are there when they are needed!

Those guards had shining weapons when they were seen in Sumatra—in the last century. And one man in particular wanted an explanation. He said to the missionary, "Now, tuan [teacher], I have yet one request."

"And what is that?"

"I would like to have a look at your watchmen close at hand."

"What watchmen do you mean? I do not have any."

"I mean the watchmen whom you station around your house at night, to protect you."

"But I have no watchmen," the missionary repeated. "I have only a little herdboy and a little cook, and they would make poor watchmen."

The man was not convinced. "May I look through

your house?" Of course he could. He searched in every corner but found no watchmen. He was disappointed. Then he explained that at first the missionary had not been welcome among his people. They had planned to kill him and his wife. He said, "We went to your house night after night; but when we came near, there stood always, close around the house, a double row of watchmen with glittering weapons, and we did not venture to attack them to get into your house."

But the angry people had not given up. They had hired a professional assassin. He laughed at their cowardice and said, "I fear no God and no devil. I will get through those watchmen easily." So they tried again one evening. The assassin went ahead, confidently swinging his weapon about his head. But he came running back and said, "No, I dare not risk it to go through alone. Two rows of big, strong men stand there, very close together, shoulder to shoulder, and their weapons shine like fire!"

"But now, tell me, tuan," said the visitor, "who are those watchmen? Have you never seen them?"

"No, I have never seen them."

"And your wife did not see them?"

"No, my wife did not see them."

"But yet we have all seen them. How is that?"

So the missionary brought his Bible and told the man about the angels and about how a loving God protects His people. And the questioner was satisfied.[2]

Again and again it has happened that way. Those guards are never off duty. And never is their help too little or too late.

Angie Bancarz tells an experience her father had. Europe was in turmoil at the time, and the streets were not especially safe. But her father often gave Bible studies in the evening. In one home, as the result of

27

these studies, a woman had been genuinely converted. But her husband was very unhappy about it.
He got a gun and threatened to kill the person he
believed had disrupted the tranquillity of their home.

Later on, however, the husband who had been so
hostile was himself converted. And he said to Angie's
father, "How is it that you had a bodyguard with you?"

"I never had a bodyguard."

"Yes, he was always with you—a uniformed soldier
with a gun strapped over his shoulder."

"No, I knew nothing about it."

Then he told Angie's father of one evening when he
had waited along the way with his gun, intending to
shoot him. But he dared not—because of the guard.[3]

Bodyguard? Uniformed soldier? Angel? Check one.

In Time of Peril

In the early days of Methodism a minister by the name of John Jones was traveling on horseback through a desolate region in northern Wales. On this particular occasion he observed a rough-looking man, armed with a reaping hook, following him on the other side of a hedge. Evidently he was aiming to accost the minister at a gate a little way ahead where it would be necessary to dismount.

John Jones realized that his life was in danger and stopped his horse for a moment of prayer. When he looked up, he saw that a man on a white horse was riding beside him. He told the stranger how relieved he was to have him come along just then but received no reply. As he continued to watch the reaper, however, he saw him emerge from his concealment and run across a field. Again he tried to make conversation with the stranger on the horse beside him, but his efforts were met with silence. Finally he said to him, "Can it for a moment be doubted that my prayer was heard and that you were sent for my deliverance by the Lord?" And the horseman responded with a single word, "Amen."

Not another word would the stranger say. But they were now approaching the gate, and the minister hurried on to dismount and open it. He waited for the man on the white horse to pass through. He didn't. He was gone. He was nowhere in sight!

He couldn't have passed through the gate. His horse could not have leaped the high hedges on either side of the road. Was it all a figment of his imagination? Had there been no horse and rider at all? But how could a figment of his imagination have frightened away the intended killer?[1]

It may come as no surprise that God protects His servants, that He sends an angel guard to surround those who love Him. But what of those who ignore Him, doubt Him, even deride Him? What of those who are His enemies? Are they always outside the circle of His care?

Says the apostle Paul, "God demonstrates his own love for us in this: While we were still sinners, Christ died for us." Romans 5:8, N.I.V.

While we were still sinners. How often our Lord has sent His angels to protect those who were still sinners—hoping to draw them, to win them, by that undeserved love!

It happened in the troubled days of the Napoleonic wars. A forester named Grimez had been instrumental in bringing to justice a band of robbers that had brought terror to the region. Only the leader of the band was still at large, and he had sworn to have his revenge upon Grimez.

The forester was not a religious man. He laughed at his wife's prayers for his safety. He preferred to trust in his weapons and his dogs.

One evening he was delayed in returning home, and his wife became anxious. Finally she brought the Bible and read aloud to the grandmother these words from the seventy-first psalm: "In thee, O Lord, do I put my trust. . . . Be thou my strong habitation. . . .

Deliver me, O my God, out of the hand of the wicked, out of the hand of the unrighteous and cruel man."

Then the two women knelt and prayed that God would protect the absent husband, and themselves, from danger. And they prayed for the robber whom they so much feared. They asked God to be merciful to him and to turn him from his evil ways.

Shortly after they rose from their knees, the husband came home. They told him of their concern and of their prayer, but he only smiled and told them it was foolish to think it did any good to pray. He checked to see that doors and windows were securely locked and that his weapons were at hand. And they all slept.

In the morning when they came downstairs, they found a window open. And on the table where the Bible had been lay a great sharp knife. The Bible was gone. Evidently someone had been in the house, and evidently the intent had been murder. The missing Bible must have had something to do with saving them, for nothing else had been taken. The wife thanked God for protection. And this time the husband did not laugh. He could see that neither his dogs nor his guns had saved them. He began to think there was something in religion after all. And the robber was never seen or heard of in that forest again.

But that isn't all the story. Some time later the French and the Prussians were fighting each other. Among those who fell was the forester, then a captain in the army. His men left him on the field, thinking he was dead. But a fisherman heard his groans and came to his aid. He then took him to his home, and he and his wife nursed him back to health.

As he was recovering, he thought much about how his life had twice been spared, even though he had been so outspoken in his unbelief. He prayed and gave his heart to the One he had so openly doubted.

When he was well enough to go home, he thanked the kind fisherman and tried to pay him for his trouble. But the fisherman refused, saying that he was actually more indebted to the forester and his wife than they were to him, and that he had something that belonged to them. He then brought out the Bible that had so mysteriously disappeared.

"I see you do not recognize me," he said, "but I am the robber that caused such trouble in your neighborhood till you caught my companions and had them put in prison. I was very angry with you for this and swore to have revenge. I crept into your house about dark one evening, intending to murder you and all your family while you were asleep. All the evening I lay under the settee in your sitting room, waiting for the hour when I could carry out my purpose. Against my will I was obliged to hear the seventy-first psalm read by your wife. It had a wonderful effect on me. When I heard her prayer, I was more affected. It seemed as if an unseen hand was laid upon me to keep me from doing what I had come to do. I felt that I could not do it. All my desire was to get that Book and read it."

He went on, "For weeks I kept it hid in the woods near your home. The Bible was my companion; and as I read it, I saw what a great sinner I was, and what a great Saviour there is in Jesus.

"You, forester, trusted to your guns and dogs; they could not have helped you any. Nothing but God's Word saved you. That was all that kept me from plunging my knife into your bosom. That was all that protected you then; it is all that has saved you from dying on the battlefield now. Don't thank me, but thank the merciful God who made use of His blessed Word to save both you and me."[2]

"While we were still sinners." Still scoffers. Still robbers.

But that undeserved care, that undeserved love, that undeserved protection is not spent on scoffers and robbers alone. How often that love has been lavished upon you and me. While we were still sinners. While we were still proud. While we thought we didn't need a Saviour. While we thought we could manage nicely on our own.

While we were still hurting Him, He was loving us. While we were disobedient, He was still kind. While we were hurtling down the path to destruction, He still protected us. While we still shunned Him, He sent His angels. Even while we refused to hear, He kept calling us back.

"Herein is love, not that we loved God, but that he loved us." 1 John 4:10.

And all of us can say, if we will, "We love him, because he first loved us." Verse 19.

Why else are the angels sent—except to draw us all into the safe and happy circle of His love?

3—I.B.A.

Sometimes a Dream

Chief Karkar, of Maramun Valley in the New Guinea hinterland, squatted on the floor of a grass hut as he related his three dreams—three dreams within a period of six days.

In his first dream, he said, he was walking along a jungle trail. Where it divided, he took a narrow trail to the right which climbed abruptly upward. For hours he plodded up the mountainside, and then, as evening approached, he found a grass shelter that appeared to be deserted. He pushed through the small doorway, happy to rest.

Out of the darkness a voice said to him, "Are you satisfied with your mission and your way of life?"

Struggling against a sudden fear, he replied, "Yes, I am quite contented with my way of life. I attend worships and meetings fairly regularly."

"But," said the voice, "you are still living much the same as you did before the mission came to your village. You still practice your heathen sing-sings and indulge in all the evils that accompany them. You still believe in talking to your evil spirits when in trouble. And let me ask you, Does your mission help you or your people when you are sick?"

He had no reply. The words were burning deep.

Then the voice spoke again, "If you want to obtain eternal life, you must follow the Seventh-day Adventist mission."

Now he was troubled. This suggestion cut across many of his practices and ambitions. He knew about the "Seven Day" mission across the valley. But he preferred his own mission, for he didn't have to give up anything to belong to it.

But once more the voice spoke. "I want you to go back to your village and tell all your people what I have told you. Then I will visit you again to see if you have done what I have asked you to do."

Awaking from sleep in his own hut, he was deeply disturbed. He decided to tell the villagers his dream—that is, a part of it. So he called them together, told them a portion of his dream, and told them he thought it meant that he would soon die. At this announcement there was hushed silence.

Two nights later he dreamed again, and the voice said in a chiding tone, "I am ashamed of you." The chief could think of nothing to say. And then after a long pause the voice said, "Why did you not give the true meaning of your dream to your people? You are not going to die. Go, tell them what I told you."

He awoke with a start. This time he hurried to take action. Even before dawn he summoned his people. This time he told them his first dream in detail, omitting nothing, and then the second dream. The people were happy as he told them he was not going to die.

Soon the whole village was astir and enthusiastic. A central site was selected for the new mission. Some of the men were sent to outposts to find the missionary's hut. And the chief himself led a delegation to visit the "Seven Day" missionary, who willingly accompanied them back to the village.

But there was one more dream for the chief. This one involved meeting a lone figure beside the path, a person who was very friendly and who told him he was building a dwelling for his villagers who would soon come to be with him. Walking on up the mountain, the chief entered the huge building. There he saw angels scurrying about, preparing a banquet. He was told that he could attend the banquet if he fulfilled the requirements.

Early the next morning he called his people together again. This time they were eager to know what he had dreamed. Among them was Warai, from the Adventist mission. He told them the true meaning of the dream—that Jesus, the Son of God, is preparing a dwelling in heaven for the faithful of all lands, that He will soon return for them, that there will be a big banquet, and that now is the time to prepare for it.

The people became very excited. Some of them began to build their huts near the new mission site, renouncing their heathen practices immediately. It was not long until 500 people were meeting together in that valley.[1]

So it is that angels, seen or unseen, prepare the way for truth. And so it is that the number of worshipers grows rapidly—worshipers who are willing to give up their heathen practices and walk where angels lead, to live clean and happy lives.

In the land of the tree dwellers, in eastern Indonesia, a man named Ranteuwa dreamed that God's true religion would come to his mountains. He dreamed that the day of worship would have special significance, that it would be neither the sixth day of the week nor the first day but the day in between. About twenty-five years later a missionary came to the village and told them of the seventh-day Sabbath. Ranteuwa remembered his dream. Some of the older villagers remembered it too, and they eagerly accepted the missionary and his stories of Jesus who died for them.[2]

Tamasombo and four of his friends, as they returned to their village in New Guinea, met a supernatural being. This being told them to change their life-style, destroy their pigs, stop chewing betel nut, clean up their village, stop traditional dances and devil worship, stop polygamy, worship on the Sabbath, and prepare for eternal life.

This was in 1963. In 1967 a man named Jerome came to their village and told them the same things. Tamasombo remembered the message given him four years before. He joined the "class ready" and was baptized a Seventh-day Adventist in 1971.[3]

Why is it, I ask, that stories like this seem to come most often from places like New Guinea, Central America, developing parts of Africa? Is God more interested, are angels more interested, in the South Pacific than the United States or Canada, England or France? Is it that people of simple living are more receptive than we who call ourselves civilized? Are they more sincere than we? Do these relatively unenlightened people treasure the little light they have while we neglect the greater light that is ours? I don't know the answer. It's something to think about.

I'm sure, however, that angels are not as unevenly distributed on this planet as it might seem. In the fall of 1971, while I was working in Washington, a friend told me of what took place only a few miles away.

A student at Columbia Union College, about four o'clock on a Friday afternoon, entered a shop in Langley Park and made some small purchase. When she came out, a sailor spoke to her. She was reluctant to enter into conversation with a stranger and tried to pass on. But he urged her to wait, saying he had something very important he must tell her. He had had a dream that impressed him very much. In that dream he had seen her come out of that particular shop with a small package and a book in her hand. He had been waiting there every afternoon that week, watching for the girl he had seen in his dream. He had been told, as I recall, that she had information he needed. And most impressive was his statement, "I am supposed to tell you that Jesus is coming sooner than you think!"

The student invited him to attend a group Bible study that evening, but he was shipping out to Germany and could not. So together they knelt on the sidewalk and prayed that God would guide each of them.

The sailor promised to look up an Adventist church in Germany as soon as possible. I do not know the rest of the story. When we talk with angels, they will fill us in on many a final chapter.[4]

Yes, angels sometimes visit—personally or in a dream—those who are seeking for truth. They also have a profoundly important message for those of us who feel secure in truth—"Jesus is coming sooner than you think!"

Sometimes a Voice

A fierce tropical storm was raging, and for a ten-year-old those storms could be sheer terror. On this particular occasion the boy was so frightened that he ran into the living room looking for some kind of protection. And there stood his father, looking out the window, completely unperturbed.

He knew how his boy felt, and he took both his hands in his. He had to lean way over so that he could be heard above the noise of the storm. And he said, "Sonny, our Father in heaven has sent His angels to be with us. Everything will be all right!"

Many times, especially in later years, Pastor John—I shall call him that—had occasion to remember his father's words and be encouraged. Many times he knew that angels were present. And on one occasion he actually heard the voice of his guardian angel.

It happened in the early sixties in a time of war. Tribes were fighting each other, and there were refugees everywhere. Pastor John was asked by a government offical to supervise the distribution of emergency supplies.

A ton of medicines was ready to be delivered. The cases had been loaded into a brand-new Dove De

Havilland, and everything was in order. But as he put his foot onto the little step that led up to the aircraft, he heard the voice of his guardian angel—heard it just as distinctly as you hear any voice. And that voice said, "No! Do not fly in that airplane!"

He didn't understand. But he obeyed. An old flying crate that was in pitiful condition was used to deliver the medicines. But the brand-new Dove De Havilland crashed on takeoff, killing everyone aboard. And Pastor John never forgot the sound of his angel's warning words![1]

It is interesting that the words spoken by angels, both as recorded in the Bible and as heard in our own modern times, are often very insistent. No! Don't do it! Get up! Hurry! Go quickly! Make haste! Those are the sort of words angels often use.

Yes, sometimes the voice of an angel has to be insistent. Otherwise we may hesitate. We may try to reason with it. But danger will not wait!

Peter Marshall, in his youth, spent a summer working in the English village of Bamburgh, sixteen miles southeast of the Scottish border. One very dark night as he was walking back to Bamburgh from a nearby village, he decided to take a shortcut. He knew that there was a deep, deserted limestone quarry in the area, but he thought he could avoid the danger spot. So he struck out across the moors. The night was starless and inky black, and the sound of the wind seemed to give it an eerie quality.

Suddenly he heard someone call, "Peter!" The voice was urgent.

He stopped. "Yes, who is it? What do you want?"

For a second he listened, but there was only the sound of the wind. Thinking he must have been mistaken, he walked on a few paces. Then he heard it again, even more urgent: *"Peter!"*

This time he stopped dead still and tried to peer into the impenetrable blackness, and suddenly he stumbled, falling to his knees. He put out his hand to catch himself, but *there was nothing there.* Cautiously he felt around in a semicircle and found that he was on the very brink of the abandoned stone quarry. Just *one more step* would have sent him plummeting to his death!

Peter Marshall never forgot that voice. And there was never any doubt in his mind about the source of it. He felt that God's intervention must mean that God had a special purpose for his life.[2]

Pastor Lloyd Wyman's father, while stationed in Burma, also heard an insistent voice. Messengers came to his home one evening, asking that he come with them to a village about two hours away where there was a great deal of sickness. He hesitated to make the trip at night because he had only a little oil in his lantern. Also a man-eating tiger had been reported in the area. So he decided to wait until morning. It would be necessary for him to get back the next evening, but the messengers promised to make the return trip with him.

He found a great deal of malaria in the village, and he did all he could for the people during the day. Toward evening, with the messengers, he started the trip home. They had gone only a little way when a voice said to him, "Light the lantern!" He turned to the others and asked, "Did you hear that?" "No." Again the voice said, "Light the lantern!" And again he asked, "Did you hear a voice?" No, they had heard no voice.

He was reluctant to light the lantern before it was really necessary because he had so little oil. But twice he had heard the voice distinctly, "Light the lantern!" So now he stopped to light it. And the moment he struck the match he understood. For there, fifteen feet ahead, right in the bend of the path, sat a tiger!

The tiger, as soon as it saw the light, ran off into the jungle. But then it turned, came back, and followed them all the way home.

And the oil did not run out![3]

It is not alone for our protection that angels speak. Sometimes it is to counsel us or to encourage us in a course of action.

Jack Circle's father, known to his friends as C.F., was a very active and dedicated layman. He was employed for a time by a portrait studio as a sales representative. And whenever possible, in the homes of prospects, he would take the opportunity to witness for his Lord, sometimes leaving a piece of literature or enrolling them in a Bible course.

One day a lady phoned the office and complained about what he was doing, and his employer told him that he must stop. C.F. was troubled about this development and didn't know just what he should do.

Not long after that he was given the name of a person interested in photographs and called at the address. On this particular morning he was very discouraged about not being able to do his witnessing. As he walked in from the street, he saw a woman at the window waving frantically, apparently at him. She was acting so strangely that he wondered if he should forget about going in. Then she threw the door open and said, "I don't know who you are or what you are doing. But a voice just spoke to me and said to tell you, 'Don't stop what you are doing!' "[4]

Is it possible that you and I, without being aware of it, have heard the voice of an angel? The Lord's special messenger wrote, "Christ and His angels come to us in the form of human beings, and as we converse with them, light and grace and joy fill our hearts. Our spiritual energies are quickened, and we are strengthened to do the will of God. Though we know it not, we are conversing with an angel, an angel in human guise."[5]

This statement intrigues me. Does it mean that angel voices speak through human beings we know, with whom we are acquainted? Or do angels, when they assume human guise, always appear as strangers to us?

Hardly had I written the question down when I discovered, from the same inspired pen, what may be the answer: "The Lord would have us understand that these mighty ones who visit our world have borne an active part in the work which we have called our own. These heavenly beings are ministering angels, and they frequently disguise themselves in the form of human beings, and *as strangers* converse with those who are engaged in the work of God. In lonely places they have been the companions of the traveler in peril. In tempest-tossed ships they have spoken words to allay fear and inspire hope in the hour of danger. Many, under different circumstances, have listened to the voices of the inhabitants of other worlds. Time and again have they been the leaders of armies. They have been sent forth to cleanse away pestilence. They have eaten at the humble board of families, and often have they appeared as weary travelers in need of shelter for the night."[6]

And then there is this thrilling statement: "Though the rulers of this world know it not, yet often in their councils angels have been spokesmen. Human eyes have looked upon them; human ears have listened to their appeals; human lips have opposed their suggestions and ridiculed their counsels; human hands have met them with insult and abuse. In the council hall and the court of justice, these heavenly messengers have shown an intimate acquaintance with human history; they have proved themselves better able to plead the cause of the oppressed than were their ablest and most eloquent defenders. They have defeated purposes and arrested evils that would have greatly retarded the work of God, and would have caused great suffering to His people."[7]

Again, these words have fascinated me for years. Do they mean that angels present in these assemblies have spoken through honest and receptive members of these assemblies? Or have angels disguised as human beings come into these assemblies *as strangers* and been allowed to speak? Would a stranger be allowed to address the United States Senate, for instance—or the United Nations? Or would an angel have to speak through a recognized member?

The experience related to me by Pastor Alger Johns offers what may be a clue, and certainly a thrilling example.

Pastor Johns, for many years a strong defender of religious liberty, was present in a Salt Lake City committee room as hearings concerning proposed Sunday legislation were in progress. The attorney who presented the case in favor of the legislation was well prepared and so powerful a speaker that our own men were dejected. It was not that we did not have strong and unassailable reasons for opposing Sunday legislation. But the witnesses scheduled to speak for us that day were weak and would certainly not be able to counteract the impression made by this dynamic speaker for the other side.

Just at that moment a stranger walked into the courtroom and asked permission to speak. He was a large man, well-dressed. He proceeded to present just the arguments needed to answer those of the speaker who had preceded him. And he did it with such power that the attorney who had made such a strong impression only moments before was confounded and simply could not continue. The stranger turned and left the courtroom, and the proposed legislation was defeated.

An effort was made to find the stranger, but he had disappeared. Who was he? Pastor Johns emphasizes that one of our own members could have been prepared by the Holy Spirit and guided into the courtroom at just the right moment. On the other hand, could it be that those present that day in the courtroom had witnessed a dramatic example of what the Lord's servant was talking about? I prefer to think it was the latter.[8]

Stand-ins

In an amazing variety of ways God uses angels to guide and protect His children. But sometimes He uses stand-ins for the angels—as when He used ravens to feed Elijah.

Pastor W. A. Spicer, in his book *The Hand That Intervenes*, a classic collection of stories of providential deliverance published in 1918, included quite a number of instances in which God used dogs, birds, and even a spider's web to protect, or provide for, His people. And of course sometimes He uses people, too, as stand-ins for the angels.

Says my favorite author, "Our heavenly Father has a thousand ways to provide for us of which we know nothing."[1]

A thousand ways. And we need only one!

In Bohemia, now a part of Czechoslovakia, a man named Dolanscious was arrested for heresy. He was imprisoned in the city of Prague, where he endured much suffering because of cruel neglect. One day, on the point of starving, he turned his eyes toward the grate of his prison window and saw a little bird sitting with something in his bill. When he tried to investigate, the bird flew away, leaving a bit of cloth. In that bit of cloth was a piece of gold, with which he was able to buy bread until he was finally released from prison.[2]

Also in Reformation days, a Protestant named Johannes Brenz was taking refuge in the home of Duke Ulric at Stuttgart. But the emperor learned of his whereabouts and commissioned a colonel to produce him dead or alive. The duke, learning of this, sent Brenz away, saying, "If God is pleased with you, He will deliver you."

In the seclusion of his room Brenz fell on his knees and prayed for guidance. And he seemed to hear a voice saying: "Take a loaf of bread, and go up through the Birkenwald [the upper part of the city]; and where you find an open front door, go in and hide yourself under the roof."

He found all the doors closed in that part of the city until he came to the Landhouse (later the Reformed church). Here the door was open. He entered and hid himself behind a large pile of wood under the roof.

The next day soldiers arrived in Stuttgart and searched every house in the city. They came to the Landhouse and searched every room. They even thrust their spears through the woodpile behind which he lay, but they did not find him. Two weeks later they left Stuttgart.

How did Brenz manage during those two weeks? On the very first day of his concealment, along toward noon, a hen came and laid an egg behind the woodpile. This she did each day. The egg quenched his thirst, and the loaf of bread satisfied his hunger. The hen stopped coming on the day the soldiers left the city.[3]

A thousand ways to provide. Remember?

In the year 1662, 2000 ministers had been ousted from the Church of England. One of them, pursued by enemies, sought refuge in a malt house and crept into the kiln. Almost immediately a spider began to weave a large and beautiful web across the narrow entrance. The web was between him and the light, and as he watched he was so fascinated by the skill of the insect weaver that he forgot his own danger. When the delicate network had crossed and recrossed the mouth of the kiln in every direction, the pursuers of the minister came in search of him. He listened as they approached and heard one of them say, "It is of no use to look in there. The old villain can never be there. Look at that spider's web. He could never have got in there without breaking it."[4]

Yes, God can use even a spider's web!

Turning to our own times, Bob Sherman tells an experience from his days in colporteuring. He felt he should make about twenty calls a day, but on one occasion he found himself in an area known for its mean dogs. At almost every house there was at least one. And they were not on leash. He could just look down the street and see the ferocious creatures he would have to encounter.

Bob did, of course, what all good colporteurs do about their problems. He prayed—prayed for both guidance and protection. And then he started out. At the first house there was no problem, nor did the dogs bother him at the second home. At the third house, as he stood talking with the lady at the door, she said to him, "Is that your dog sitting out there?"

He turned to look. There was this very large dog, a sort of English-bulldog type. He was just sitting there, not barking. But his appearance was such that a person would think twice before encountering him needlessly. And apparently the neighborhood dogs shared that feeling, for they did not approach him.

He told the woman he had never seen the dog before. Neither had she.

At the next house it was the same. "Is that your dog sitting out there?" And so on down the street. The dog followed him from house to house, quietly waiting, as if he were on guard. The neighborhood dogs didn't come near. No one knew where the strange dog came from. And when Bob had finished at the last house, the dog disappeared.[5]

As if he were on guard? Maybe he was. Evidently he was! Did an angel put him there?

And then there is the story of Brownie—a smelly, snarly, stubborn dog. The pastor's wife was returning from a meeting late at night. Her husband was out of town, and she and the children were alone. She let herself in quietly and was surprised to find the kitchen light on, with Ted studying at the table. They commented briefly about the wet weather. Then she looked down and gasped. There was Brownie, their huge, mangy dog, stretched out at Ted's side!

"Ted! What's Brownie doing in the house? You know he's never stayed inside before!"

Ted looked up and shrugged. "He just wanted in, so I let him in. Then I decided I might as well bring my homework down here."

Brownie wanted in! That was utterly incongruous. So was everything else about the dog. Black, brown, and smelly, he wandered to the parsonage one day and just decided to stay. He adopted the family, became fiercely protective of every one of them, loved them so much he wanted to be wherever they were—anywhere except inside. When they brought him inside, he exhibited a severe claustrophobia. He would race in terror from door to door and window to window till they let him out. No amount of coaxing or bribing could keep him in.

Until now. There he was, lying calmly in the kitchen like an ordinary house dog!

49

Shaking her head, she went down to the basement to bolt the door leading to the outside. She came back up. Ted had gone to bed, and she was ready for sleep too. But better put Brownie out first.

Brownie refused to budge. The pastor's wife wheedled and coaxed, pushed and pulled, tried to bribe him to the door with a piece of meat. He wouldn't move. She picked up his hind end and yanked him toward the door and out of it. Like quicksilver, she says, his front end slid back in. And so it went. She gave up, shut all the doors to the kitchen, and went wearily to bed.

The next morning Brownie reverted to his true nature and tore frantically out of the house. Still puzzled, wondering why the dog had been so determined to stay in the night before, she started downstairs to turn on the furnace. At the bottom of the stairs she felt a breath of cold, damp air. And then a wave of panic hit her. The outside door was open!

Was someone in the basement? No. She had bolted the door. Someone had *gone out* of the basement. Someone *had been* in the basement—had been there when she went down to bolt the door!

Now it all made sense. Whoever was in the basement had heard her noisy and unsuccessful attempt to get Brownie out. And he knew that he would have to come up through the kitchen and encounter that stubborn dog—or else just go back out the way he had come in!

Had the Lord given their guardian angel, instead of glorious, dazzling wings, four stubborn, mangy feet on that wild, stormy night, as she suggests? I would prefer to say that Brownie was a smelly, snarly, stubborn but effective stand-in![6]

And then God uses brave men, too, as stand-ins for the angels.

George Buttrick tells the story of a hero of the Chinese rice fields. It happened during an earthquake. From his hilltop farm he saw the ocean swiftly pull back, like some ferocious animal crouching for the leap. And he knew that the leap would be the tidal wave. He saw too that his neighbors working in the fields below must somehow be brought to his hill—and fast—or be swept away!

His own rice had already been harvested. There it was, still in the husks, the cut plants piled in huge stacks—practically his total food supply. But without a moment's hesitation he set fire to the stacks and furiously rang the temple bell. His neighbors thought his farm was on fire and rushed to help him. Then, from that safe hill, they looked down and saw the water swirling over the fields they had just left—and knew how much their rescue had cost![7]

Yes, God alone, from His high eternity, could see the tidal wave of sin crouched, ready to rush in and sweep us away.

He knew that only a Sacrifice could save us. And so He set heaven afire with His own love, made a daring descent to earth, and climbed upon a cross to die!

And only when we flee to the high safety of that cross, drawn by that incredible fire that lights up all the ages—only then can we look back and see the depth and the fury of the ruin from which He saved us. And understand the cost!

Jesus said, "And I, if I be lifted up from the earth, will draw all men unto me."

And for those who linger in the low fields, unaware of danger, there is still the insistent ringing of the bell!

Replay

Bible times were exciting times. Miracles everywhere. Angels scurrying about, always appearing just at the right time. Ready to push over Jericho's walls or lead Peter out of prison or make a way for Jesus through an angry mob. Elijah fed by ravens. His prayer turning off the rain. The fiery furnace. The lions' den. What a time to live!

So when the Scriptures were finished, angels were tired and began to take it easy. Miracles were put on the shelf. Prayers were stacked up and neglected. God can't do for us what He did for the people back there.

Is that the way it was—and is? Don't ever think it!

"The Lord's hand is not shortened, that it cannot save; neither his ear heavy, that it cannot hear." Isaiah 59:1.

And Jesus Christ is "the same yesterday, and to day, and for ever." Hebrews 13:8.

We have already seen that God still has ravens—and dogs and hens and spiders—that do His bidding. Even as you read these words, God is hearing prayers—and answering them in ways as spectacular as in the days of Elijah. And before you finish these pages, you will read a modern variation of the fiery furnace story that will take your breath away!

The truth is that God and His angels are ready with a replay of the miracles of Bible times wherever they are needed!

Says the Lord's servant, "All that Christ received from God we too may have. Then ask and receive. With the persevering faith of Jacob, with the unyielding persistence of Elijah, claim for yourself all that God has promised."[1]

But you say, "Elijah was a great man. I can't expect God to do for me what He did for Elijah. I'm just an ordinary person."

Yes, Elijah was a great man—when he was guided and strengthened and controlled by the power of God. He was a great man atop Mount Carmel. But only hours later, when he withdrew his hand from the hand of God, he was very, very ordinary—fleeing in fear from Jezebel's threats, dejected, depressed, wanting to die.

"Elijah was a man subject to like passions as we are, and he prayed earnestly that it might not rain: and it rained not on the earth by the space of three years and six months. And he prayed again, and the heaven gave rain, and the earth brought forth her fruit." James 5:17, 18.

God's promises are for us. His miracles are for us. His angels are watching over us. Every one of us. You and me. Listen to these words from the servant of the Lord:

"When in faith we take hold of His strength, He will change, wonderfully change, the most hopeless, discouraging outlook. He will do this for the glory of His name."[2]

"Living faith in the Redeemer will smooth the sea of life, and will deliver us from danger in the way that He knows to be best."[3]

"Nothing can stand in His way. His power is absolute, and it is the pledge of the sure fulfilment of His promises to His people. . . . He has means for the removal of every difficulty, that those who serve Him and respect the means He employs may be delivered."[4]

These stories of angel activity are not brought together to entertain you. They are to strengthen your faith. They are to deepen your conviction that "with God all things are possible." Matthew 19:26.

We are tempted, sometimes, to think that Jesus had an advantage over us, that He could live as He lived because of who He was. He was divine. He had powers that we do not have. He could do things we cannot do.

But inspiration tells us, "Jesus revealed no qualities, and exercised no powers, that men may not have through faith in Him."[5]

Jesus could walk through an angry mob and disappear. We can't do that.

But angels led John Wesley through an angry mob.[6] They did the same for Dr. Adam Clarke, author of *Clarke's Commentary*.[7] An angel led James White through an angry mob.[8]

These men were great leaders, you say. Yes, but listen to this contemporary incident involving an Adventist minister, his wife, and a young Jewish girl who had become interested in the Adventist faith. As the two ladies were distributing literature a husky agitator began a loud tirade of verbal abuse. The Adventist minister, sensing danger, confronted the agitator, who said, "Who are you?"

"I am her husband," he replied. Listen as the pastor's wife tells it: "Then all fury broke loose. Satan seemed to have full control of the man. In his rage, he began pummeling my husband and at the same time yelling at the top of his voice. For the first time I realized the seriousness of the situation. In my dis-

54

tress, despite the fact that I was pressed in on every side by Jewish people, I lifted up my voice to Heaven and audibly called, 'Jesus, help us.'

"As I did this, something impelled me to look back, where to my great astonishment, I saw an empty lane leading to the road, as though someone had gone through the crowd and had ordered the people to pull to one side. There was no policeman in sight. I walked through the open space, the Jewish girl followed me, and my husband followed her, unnoticed and unmolested by the crowd. The angel of the Lord must have hidden us from view, for that troublemaker stayed behind still breathing out his invectives."[9]

Jesus had power over nature. He could command the wind and the waves to be still. We can't.

But angels still have that power. They are constantly executing replays of the miracles of Jesus—sometimes in refreshing and unexpected variation. For when an angel says, "Freeze!" fire or flood or hail, runaway horses or speeding cars—or stolen carabao (water buffalo)—will stop as dead still as Balaam's donkey!

Jeanette Snorrason was driving down the left lane of a busy street. Ahead of her a car was flashing its left-turn signal. Hoping to avoid a delay, she checked to see if the right lane was clear and then turned her wheels to enter it. That is, she tried to turn the wheels. They would not turn. They seemed to be locked. At that moment a sports car, which she had not seen, came speeding by in the lane she had tried to enter. Who locked the wheels?[10]

Einar Thuesen was driving a team of four horses home from a wheat field. They were young and lively and eager to get home. He let them trot along. But suddenly an open newspaper blew up under them, and they panicked. They began running as fast as they could—and he could not stop them. What could he do but pray? He had hardly begun his prayer when the horses stopped as if they had run up against a stone wall. They would not go ahead one step nor to the side. They were jumping up and down and were shaking from fright.[11]

Who stopped those horses? Was this a replay of Balaam's donkey?

Samuel Llamos lives on a mountain farm in the Philippines. One night his only carabao was stolen, and he was unable to find it. He could only pray and leave the matter in God's hands. At the end of four weeks he was asked to go to San Carlos to identify a carabao. The animal recognized him immediately, ran to greet him, and began licking his hand.

The man who stole the carabao had gone halfway to the market, Samuel learned, when suddenly the carabao stopped. No matter how much the man whipped the animal, it would not move. Why?[12]

Muriel Wichman and Alice Kuhn were crossing the mountains, when the car skidded on the ice and began spinning in wider and wider circles. Suddenly the car was picked up and set down, dead still on the ice, just to the right of center, headed in the right direction. Who did it?[13]

But I must tell you about Duane Tank. His story seems to fit here, though I'm not sure why. It is hardly a simple replay of Balaam's donkey, or of the Spirit snatching away Philip, or David escaping the spear of Saul. It has overtones of all three. But this is what happened.

Duane and his wife had attended prayer meeting in Redwood City, California, one evening and were driving home, heading toward Mountain View. They had been married about two years at the time. In those days the road was a three-lane highway, with the middle lane used for passing. There was little traffic that night, with only a few cars on the road. They were almost to Dinah's Shack, a restaurant, when Duane pulled into the middle lane, which was clear, to pass another car.

But suddenly a car zipped out from behind an approaching car into the middle lane and headed right for them. The driver seemed not to see them at all. Duane could not possibly move into another lane, because he was now even with a car on both sides. There was literally no place to go—a Red Sea situation, maybe that's it. In just seconds the two cars were approaching each other at fifty or sixty miles an hour and were headlight to headlight, possibly fifty feet apart!

Philip was set down at Azotus. Duane and his wife were set down in the Dinah's Shack parking lot. That's where they were—the next thing they knew—just turning around in the lot. There were no skid marks!

How did they get there? Did angels pick them up—car and all—and move them over the other car? Or cause the other car to disappear? Did angels make a safe lane through traffic—as at the Red Sea? Or just snatch them up and set them down? They don't know. It may be that in this case the angels executed a triple play too fast for the understanding![14]

The day of miracles is not past. God could even today rerun the Jonah or the Daniel chapters to save lives and strengthen the faith of His dear people.

Out on a Limb

How far out on a limb should faith go? How far *can* it go without falling straight into the waiting arms of presumption?

One of the best-known instances of spiritual daring, of course, is that of George Müller and the fog. Here it is again, as remembered by the captain of the ship, whose own Christian life was revolutionized by the experience.

The captain had been on the bridge for twenty-two hours without leaving it when he was startled by someone tapping him on the shoulder. It was George Müller. "Captain," he said, "I have come to tell you that I must be in Quebec on Saturday afternoon." This was Wednesday.

The captain replied without hesitation, "It is impossible."

"I have never broken an engagement for fifty-seven years."

"I would willingly help you. How can I? I am helpless."

"Let us go down to the chart room and pray."

"I never heard of such a thing. Mr. Müller, do you know how dense this fog is?"

"No," he replied, "my eye is not on the density of

the fog but on the living God, who controls every circumstance of my life."

So they went to their knees, and the man of God prayed a very simple prayer. The captain muttered to himself that it might be suitable for a class of eight- or ten-year-olds. It was something like this: "O Lord, if it is consistent with Thy will, please remove this fog in five minutes. You know the engagement You made for me in Quebec for Saturday. I believe it is Your will."

The captain was going to pray, but Müller put his hand on his shoulder and told him not to. He said, "First, you do not believe He will; and, second, I believe He has, and there is no need whatever for you to pray about it."

The captain looked at him, amazed. And he continued, "Captain, I have known my Lord for fifty-seven years, and there has never been a single day that I have failed to gain an audience with the King. Get up, captain, and open the door, and you will find the fog is gone."

He got up, and the fog was gone![1]

What a faith! But more importantly, What a God!

Now, George Müller was not a man who made a practice of praying for strange or unreasonable things. But in his deep conviction that God was going to work this miracle, he felt confident in laying both his faith and God's power on the line in this very open way. Surely God would not have worked as He did if the request had been tainted with presumption.

"These signs shall follow them that believe," said Jesus. "In my name shall they cast out devils; they shall speak with new tongues; They shall take up serpents; and if they drink any deadly thing, it shall not hurt them; they shall lay hands on the sick, and they shall recover." Mark 16:17, 18.

These words have often been fulfilled. More often

they have been so misunderstood as to be considered a license for showmanship.

You recall how "when Paul had gathered a bundle of sticks, and laid them on the fire, there came a viper out of the heat, and fastened on his hand." Acts 28:3.

The island people watched for him to die, but "he shook off the beast into the fire, and felt no harm."

But remember that Paul had not created this emergency. It was an accident. He did not pick up the viper and say, "Look what I can do!"

And then there is the case of Miss Annie Taylor, who entered the forbidden land of Tibet in the year 1890, working there for a time in spite of all efforts to keep her out, to put her out, and to starve her out. The people kept asking her what to do with her body if she died, and she told them she wasn't going to die right then. Finally poison was put in the food she was invited to eat. Her suspicion was aroused almost immediately, and it was not long till she became ill, with all the symptoms of aconite poisoning. She felt her strength going; her heart was slowing. And then, through the window, she saw that a crowd was silently gathering. She realized that they had come in curiosity to watch her die.

There she was, alone in a strange and hostile land. But her Lord was with her, and she remembered and claimed His promise—for the sake of Tibet. Immediately she felt the blood tingling again in her veins. Her heart became normal, and her strength returned. She took her Tibetan Scripture portion and went outside to preach Jesus and His power to save to those who had come to see her die![2]

I think you see that there is one thing that stands out in all these experiences. These servants of their Lord did not create these emergencies. What a far cry from the cheap showmanship becoming so prevalent today—with snakes deliberately handled, poison purposely imbibed, insulin stopped, medical help refused, just to show what people can do or what faith can do or what God can do! And the Lord Jesus Christ, in whose name it is done, has nothing to do with it. It is no wonder that senseless, pitiful, unnecessary tragedies have resulted!

There is a wide place for faith, even daring faith. But presumption lurks close by. And the line between is very thin. Only those who walk very close to their Lord will know where that line is.

If God sees fit to bring us into a tight place so that He can demonstrate His power to get us out, that is His business. We are told that "God in his providence brought the Hebrews into the mountain fastnesses before the [Red] sea, that He might manifest His power in their deliverance."[3]

Yes even Jesus "would not place Himself, unbidden, in a position that would necessitate the interposition of His Father to save Him from death. He would not force Providence to come to His rescue, and thus fail of giving man an example of trust and submission."[4] He was living as we have to live, as our Example. And "He would not, at Satan's suggestion, tempt God by presumptuously experimenting on His providence."[5]

Shall we step out by faith? By all means. Even way out if necessary? Yes. But presumptuously experiment? Never!

Not many years ago a story filtered out from a certain Eastern European country. You understand, of course, that there is no way to check the accuracy of a story that reaches us by way of many tellings. Yet certainly there is no reason why it could not have happened just as it is told.

A Christian worker, according to this account, had

been arrested and imprisoned. One day he was taken from his cell and led into an interrogation room where a police officer and a doctor were sitting at a table. Lying open on the table was a Bible, and the prisoner was asked if he believed that book to be the Word of God. He answered that he did. Then he was asked to read Mark 16:18. And he read aloud, "And if they drink any deadly thing, it shall not hurt them."

"Do you believe this part of the Bible too?" the officer demanded. And the Christian replied, "Yes."

The officer then placed a filled glass on the table and said, "In this glass there is a strong poison. If the book is true, as you insist, it won't hurt you. But to show you we don't play with you, watch this!"

A large dog was brought in and given some of the liquid. In a very few moments the dog was dead.

"Do you still claim that this book you call 'God's Word' is true?"

"Yes, it is God's Word. It is true."

Then, with the doctor looking on, the officer shouted, "Drink the entire glass!"

The Christian asked permission to pray first. He knelt down by the table, took the glass in his hands, and prayed for his family that their faith might not fail. Then he prayed for the officer and the doctor that they too might become followers of Christ. Then he said, "Lord, You see how they have challenged You. I am ready to die. But I believe Your Word that nothing will happen to me. Should Your plan be different, I am ready to meet You. My life is in Your hands. May Your will be done."

Then he lifted the glass and drank it down. The doctor and the officer were amazed and not a little surprised. They hadn't expected this. They thought he would break first. Now they watched for him to collapse. He didn't. There was complete silence. The minutes seemed like hours. Finally the doctor made the first move. He felt the prisoner's pulse. It was normal. He continued his examination but could find no symptoms, no evidence of harm. He couldn't hide his astonishment. At last he slumped into his chair, paused a moment, then took his party card from his pocket, tore it in half, and threw it on the floor!

Then he reached out for the Bible, took it in his hand, and held it reverently. "From today," he said with conviction, "I too will believe this Book. It must be true. I too am ready to believe this Christ who did this thing before my eyes!"[6]

But I must share one more experience—one that is an amazing demonstration of faith and of angel intervention. The story has special appeal because it happened not to an experienced worker for Christ, not to a great Christian leader, but to a young girl who loved her Lord and knew that He loved her.

During the fearful Mau Mau incidents in Kenya, East Africa, in the 1950s, many African Christians were persecuted and tortured because of their identification with what some considered to be a foreign religion. Mau Mau leaders were trying to force all Africans to take an oath that involved obscene acts and a promise to worship the leader of the Mau Mau.

Gakui, a teenage girl who had been at our mission school only a year, determined that she would not take the oath. Her parents coaxed her, and the Mau Mau threatened her with death if she refused. And then one day she was seized and taken to the ceremonial hut.

"Will you take the oath?" they demanded.

"I cannot," she replied. "I am a Christian."

They slapped her face. "Do you want to die?"

And she said, "I don't want to die, and I know Jesus will save me. I know He will!"

At that they beat her until she fell unconscious to

the floor. Then they dragged her body over to the wall, because there were other young people to take the oath. Gradually she regained consciousness and watched in horror as these youth performed filthy acts and swore the terrible oath.

She prayed, "O God, save me, save me!" And as she prayed she felt strong hands grip her feet. She was pulled slowly but steadily through a hole in the wall. Once outside, she rose slowly to her feet, and then, unnoticed, she slipped away to the home of a Christian family where she was hidden until the trouble was over.

Government officials then examined the hut and could find no sign whatever of the hole through which she had been pulled!

And when the officials asked her to identify her tormentors and place charges against them, she said quietly, "No, I do not want to do that. They did not realize what they were doing. I have hope that they will be Christians someday!"[7]

What a faith! As daring as that of Daniel and the three Hebrews. And what a sweet, forgiving spirit! Like that of Jesus and Stephen. Heaven must have been pleased beyond measure!

Sometimes I Wonder

I've never seen an angel. That is, I don't know that I have. But sometimes I wonder if I gave three of them a ride one stormy night a long time ago.

It was the night I drove from San Diego to Santa Barbara in the very worst of a southern California flood. My daughter Judy, two or three years old, slept through most of the trip in the backseat. Most everything that could happen was happening, or so it seemed. At one point the highway was closed, but I was told how to go around and get back on. In one town—or city—I drove through three blocks of water so deep it was gushing around the headlights. Abandoned cars were all around me, and the old Durant I was driving stalled but started again. I couldn't have paid for towing. I had about 75 cents, and the trip was taking twice the usual time.

I pushed another car several blocks to a service station. That was no problem. So when, shortly after that, three men hailed me and wanted to be pushed to a station, I could see no reason to refuse—at least not in a storm like that. It was about two or three in the morning by then.

This time it was twenty miles before we came to a station that was open. Three of those miles were

65

through water that looked like a lake. I have no idea how those three men could tell where the highway was. But all I had to do was push.

When we did come to a station that was open, the men filled my tank with gas. Then they asked if they could ride with me into Los Angeles. Their car's motor was wet, and they wanted to leave it at the station to dry out. This was the most providential thing that could have happened, for I did not know my way through Los Angeles even when it wasn't flooded. I had intended to go directly up the coast and bypass the city, but I had missed the sign in the storm.

These three men knew exactly which streets were flooded and exactly how to avoid them. We didn't have to backtrack once. One got out of the car at one point, another farther on, and the third man got out just a block from Wilshire Boulevard. From there I knew my way.

It didn't occur to me at the time, but in the intervening years I have often wondered if those three men may have been angels. Of course God uses men too. But still I wonder!

I must tell you about George Pease. I wrote a letter to him once. And he didn't read it the way I wrote it. I've always wondered if an angel altered it.

It happened this way. I had written a song called "Jesus, Take My Hand." One evening while I was praying, I felt very definitely impressed that I should have it printed and that I should ask an aunt of mine for the money needed. This seemed very strange, for I knew my aunt had no money to spare. I asked her anyway—the impression had been so strong—and she said, "Ask George Pease. I think he would help you."

George Pease, an old family friend, was living in a hotel in downtown Portland. When I called the hotel, I learned he was in Seattle, and I wrote him there.

Now I knew that I would need about fifty dollars to have plates made of the song and have it printed. But this was at a time when I was not working. It was also at a time when fifty dollars was a huge amount of money. I simply could not bring myself to ask for fifty dollars, so I asked for twenty-five and prayed that he would send fifty.

He wrote back immediately and enclosed a check for fifty dollars. He said, "You asked for forty-five, and for the extra five you can send me whatever copies you think I can understand and appreciate."

I asked for forty-five? My handwriting is not the best, but this figure was clearly written out, and there was no possible way "twenty-five" could look like "forty-five."

Did an angel change it? I don't know. But I have always wondered.

Then there was the time I prayed that an angel would go into a printshop and change the color on some printing that had already been done. At least I couldn't think of any other way my problem could be solved.

It was no life-or-death matter at all. I was having a little booklet of poems printed. It was called *Tangled Threads;* and an artist friend had done some borders for me that were to be printed in a very delicate tint—just atmosphere, really. As I stopped by at the printshop, the borders were on the press, and the run half finished. But the borders were not a delicate tint. They were just the opposite—too dark and too bold. I was heartsick. But the printer would not see it as any great calamity. I could hardly demand a rerun. And what can you do about something that is already done?

Most people are sensible enough not to pray about what is already done. To use a Bible example, David prayed and wept over his baby for seven days. And when the baby died, he stopped praying. But I wasn't David. I went home and prayed and wept for about two hours—over something that was already done!

And what happened? Did an angel go and change those borders? No. But the printer ran out of ink before the run was finished. He had to mix more, and it didn't match. Having differing borders across the page from each other was hardly acceptable; so he decided to do the entire run over. They were printed as I wanted them.

A thousand ways to solve our difficulties— remember? Even when it may seem too late to pray.

Experiences like that have meant a great deal to me—especially because they show that God is interested not alone in life-threatening situations, but in the seemingly insignificant things that concern us.

But there were the other kind too. Angels must have been around when at the age of seven I had my tonsils removed in a small-town doctor's office—and the doctor said I died. (I didn't go through any dark tunnels or see my body on the table or anything like that.)

They must have been close by on the day I was out walking not far from Walla Walla College and some men across a field were shooting geese or something—and I felt the wind of a bullet just above my head. They surely were on duty the day I was in a serious automobile collision—and escaped without a scratch. And I *know* they were close at hand when at the age of seventeen I was miraculously healed in answer to prayer!

There was the time I didn't see an angel. But others said they did—hovering over an evening prayer band in which I was kneeling. I thought it might have been imagination. But fifteen years later I received a letter from someone whose name I did not recognize— someone who had been profoundly affected by the memory of seeing that figure of light.

I must tell you one more experience. I don't know just how or if angels were involved. But it seems to me they must have been—in some way. It happened in the city of Portland. I had been praying that some music plates made in Chicago would arrive in time to get the songs printed to take with me on a trip Monday morning. It came up to Sunday, the day before, and they had not arrived, though I did have word that they had been sent by express. But did you ever try to get something out of an express office on Sunday?

All morning I kept calling the main office and the branch office without results. About one or two o'clock the branch office closed for the day, and the main office expected nothing more in from Chicago. I think I was surprised more than disappointed, for I had really expected my prayer to be answered. But nothing more could be done; so Judy and I took an interurban that ran between Portland and Gladstone, where the Oregon camp meeting was in session.

Just after a stop along the way, a girl came and sat down beside me. She had been dozing, she said, and then, roused by the stop, she looked around and saw me. I knew her only as Mary. She had frequently come to the office of "The Quiet Hour" program and helped with mailing as a volunteer. I knew nothing else about her. But she said, "There's a package for you down at the office."

I had the strange feeling that someone had been looking over my shoulder all morning. "What office?" I asked. And she said, "The express office. It came in about eleven o'clock."

Judy and I got off at the next stop, went back into Portland, got the plates, and took them to the printer, who printed the songs that night. I took them with me the next morning, with the ink still not completely dry.

The remarkable thing about all this is that Mary was the *only person in the world* who both knew me and knew where that package was. And God put us on the same interurban!

And again, I treasure this sort of experience because it shows that God is interested in everything that concerns us, whether or not it involves great danger or any threat to life. He is concerned with the little things too!

I don't mean to give the impression that all the special experiences in my life, with or without angels, took place years ago. There is hardly a day that I don't feel the presence of those patient celestial beings—or see some undeniable evidence that they have been around. But you wouldn't want to read a book a foot thick, would you? And yet it didn't seem quite right to share so many experiences from the lives of others and not include a few pages from my own.

I know I weary the angels sometimes. I hope I haven't wearied you. But I just wanted to tell you.

The Touch of
Angel Hands

David Duffie, his high fever in its second day, had just asked Daisy to get down the big medical book and look up under bubonic plague.

Daisy looked at her young doctor husband in terror. "Bubonic plague! You don't think it's bubonic plague, do you, David?"

She read aloud from the book, her voice trembling: "Bubonic plague may be carried by infected rodents. . . . Incubation period, one to six days. . . . Onset of illness is sudden, usually accompanied by high fever. . . . The first swelling appears on lymph node nearest site of inoculation. . . . Generalized swelling throughout lymphatic system follows. . . . Disease is endemic to Lake Titicaca area—"

Everything fitted. On Monday David had finally secured permission to remove his medical books from the rat-infested warehouse in Puno where they had been stored. Friday afternoon a slight swelling under his left arm. That evening a temperature of 104 degrees. Just a bad case of flu, he thought. Saturday night, the swelling now general, he first noticed the tiny telltale scratch on his hand and remembered the rat-infested warehouse. That's when he became suspicious.

Daisy read on silently, through stinging tears: "A crisis to be reached fifth or sixth day after onset of illness. . . . Can expect either improvement or turn for the worse. . . . Little hope after patient is in coma stage. . . . Coma deepens until death." She knew that bubonic plague was usually fatal. But then, as she read on, there was a little hope: "Sulfadiazine in large doses sometimes helpful. . . . Antibubonic serum, if given early in the course of the disease."

Of course! Antibubonic serum! She fairly leaped to her feet. She would start the sulfa immediately. She would cable Lima for the serum. Dr. Potts would come from Lima. Everything would be all right!

The cablegram was sent. It read, "Dr. Duffie. Bubonic plague. Send antibubonic serum. Urgent. Please reply."

Then she waited. Waited for the serum. Waited for the fever to drop. Waited for Dr. Potts to come. Waited for everything. Sunday passed, and Monday. Tuesday morning and still no word. In the meantime she did everything she could. But nothing brought down the fever or relieved the pain.

On Tuesday afternoon, however, there seemed to be a change. David was quieter and in less pain. He could even sleep some. It seemed the crisis had passed. Daisy was relieved—until she realized what it all meant. The change was not for the better at all. David was beginning to slip into a coma!

Now she sent a second cablegram, this time paying extra so that it would be delivered to Dr. Potts's home and signed for. (Later she would learn that the first cablegram was never received at all. The second was promptly delivered to his home and signed for at the door by the maid. Dr. Potts was not at home, and the maid put the urgent cablegram in a top dresser drawer where the doctor found it two days later.)

72

Wednesday morning David could not take food or swallow. It was difficult to arouse him. Soon he was completely unconscious.

At 2:00 p.m. the clinic personnel gathered for special prayer for their doctor. And then Noel, the Argentine nurse, started out in his little Ford for the secondary school seven kilometers away. He would bring back a group of ministers and teachers for a special service of prayer and anointing.

Daisy, at two o'clock, was sitting at David's bedside. She could scarcely discern his breathing, and she noticed that fluid was beginning to form on his lungs. The words of the twenty-third psalm flashed into her mind: "Though I walk through the valley of the shadow of death, I will fear no evil: for thou art with me." But in her despair she couldn't help asking silently, "Is God with me in this hour? Does He hear? Why, oh, why has He not sent help?"

At that moment there was a knock at the door. It was Marcilino with word of an emergency at the clinic. A patient was hemorrhaging, and Noel was gone. Could she please come?

She told Marcilino to sit by the bed with his hand on David's pulse and let her know instantly if there was any change. She hurried out. The emergency was serious and took longer than she had expected.

Forty-five minutes later she rushed back into the house. Marcilino was sitting on the sofa in the living room, nonchalantly leafing through a *National Geographic* magazine. She was indignant, and she was terrified. Both at once. Why had the usually dependable Marcilino disobeyed her instructions? Why was he in the living room? Had the terrible moment come while she was gone?

The boy was utterly mystified at her outbreak. Hesitatingly he tried to explain why he had deserted the doctor. "The doctor told me to go out," he said simply.

"The doctor told you?" She choked now. "The doctor hasn't spoken for two days!" She couldn't say another word. Tremblingly she pushed open the closed door, terrified at the thought of what she would find.

The bed was empty. In front of the dresser stood David, fully dressed, his stethoscope in hand!

"David Duffie, what are you doing?" she gasped.

"Oh, thought I'd better go over to the clinic and make rounds," he said pleasantly. "Haven't seen the patients for several days, have I? What day is it, anyway?"

When the troubled little group of teachers arrived at three o'clock for the special prayer and anointing service, they were ushered into the clinic consultation room for a time of special thanksgiving. Dr. Duffie sat at the desk.

A look at Marcilino's careful notes revealed this: "2:20, doctor turned over in bed. 2:25, he asked me what I wanted and told me I could go."

It was at 2:20 that Noel had reached the school with the sad news. The men had dropped immediately to their knees![1]

Where is the angel in this remarkable story of healing? Interestingly enough, this is what we read from the servant of the Lord: "The miracles of Christ for the afflicted and suffering were wrought by the power of God through the ministration of the angels. And it is through Christ, by the ministration of His heavenly messengers, that every blessing comes from God to us."[2]

In the case of David and Daisy Duffie, all human help had failed. Cablegrams had been no help. The medicine had not come. The doctor from Lima had not come. But the unconscious doctor and his despairing wife were not alone. They were not without help. The touch of angel hands, directed by the Great Healer, had restored David instantly to health.

The experience of Nondis, a boy of New Guinea, is equally remarkable, though very different.

When a messenger burst into the village of Papua with word that the government patrol was approaching, the people fled in terror. They had never seen white men before, and they were taking no chances. Mothers scooped up their babies; and everybody, young and old, disappeared into the bush or up the mountain. Everybody, that is, except Nondis. He couldn't go, because he was crippled with leprosy!

So when the patrol officers trudged wearily into the village, they found houses empty, cooking fires still burning, and Nondis. Imagine, if you can, his absolute terror as a strange white man in a big hat bent over him and examined him.

Within a week the boy, who knew nothing of the rest of the world, was put aboard a strange aircraft and taken to a leprosarium on the coast. There he was operated upon and sealed in plaster from the soles of his feet to the top of his hips. Think of the trauma of it. No friends. No one could understand his language. He sat alone on his bed day after day, unable even to feed himself because his arms were so deformed.

It was in this condition that an Adventist pastor found him and became his friend. He brought him food and clothing, and slowly Nondis learned to speak pidgin. Now the pastor could tell him about Jesus and how He restored the paralytics and healed the lepers. He told him that Jesus is the same today. And the boy believed!

Three months after the plaster was applied, it was cut away. But his joints were still weak and twisted.

75

His left leg was badly ulcerated. It was a terrible disappointment. Now he must be encased in plaster again, this time for six months. But the pastor encouraged him to keep trusting. He told him Jesus still could heal him. And Nondis believed it was true and kept on praying.

On the second Monday night after Nondis was sealed in plaster the second time, he had a dream. In his dream a tall Man in shining white stood by his bed and said to him, "Nondis, it's time for you to get out of bed."

He said, "I can't. Look at me!"

But the Man said kindly, "You *can!* Give Me your hand."

Nondis held out his wasted hand. But the Man said, "No! Open your fingers like this."

"It's not possible. You see, my motor nerves have died, and my hand is permanently disfigured." That's what he had heard the doctors say.

"If you take My hand, your own will straighten." And, in the dream, it was so.

Then the Man in white said kindly, "Now come, get out of bed."

So in his dream Nondis swung his legs over the side of his hospital bed and stood up.

"Go for a walk." And he strode off down the ward.

When he came back to his bed, the Man in the dream said to him, "You have been sick a long time since you first believed, yet your belief in Me hasn't wavered at all. Tonight I have taken away your leprosy and have restored your movement. Now I want you to work for Me."

Nondis said he would, and thanked the Man profusely as He turned and left the room.

Not long after that the boy was awakened by the sound of a patient down the ward calling out. A nurse turned on the light. It was almost dawn anyway, and Nondis decided to say his morning prayer. But in the midst of his prayer he remembered his dream.

Nondis opened his eyes and could hardly believe what he saw. His fingers were straight. He opened both hands several times. It was easy. He examined his formerly twisted arms. He could move them!

Next he felt for his legs. He was happily shocked to discover that the plaster had all crumbled away. The sores had healed, and his joints were strong and firm. Overjoyed, he slipped out of bed and fell to his knees. How could he thank his Lord enough?

When a male nurse passed by, Nondis called him and showed him his hands and his legs. The nurse was astounded at the sight of Nondis standing. The nurse called the other patients to come and see. Excitedly they crowded around him. But some said he shouldn't have removed the plaster. When the doctor came, he cleared that up, however, telling them it was utterly impossible for Nondis to remove the plaster when he couldn't even feed himself.

The doctor examined the boy and said, "I think your God has had something to do with this."

X rays of his legs were proof of his remarkable healing. Blood tests were negative. Nondis was cleared to return home. But he said to his doctor, "The Lord said I should work for Him, but I really don't know what kind of work I should do. Can you give me some work?"

So Nondis was put to work in the physiotherapy department. That was the beginning. Soon he was transferred to an Adventist hospital, was baptized, and married a lovely Christian girl named Rebecca.[3]

Yes, angels are often sent on missions of healing. But sometimes the Healer is so moved with compassion that He takes charge Himself!

They Also Care

The Wyman family were in Calcutta at the time. Ruth was three years old. She doesn't remember anything about the experience in which she was involved. But this is the story as her parents told it to her.

They were living on the top floor of an apartment house, probably the third floor. Her parents had a Bible-study appointment with a family down on the first floor that evening, and for some reason they had no baby-sitter. Since they would be in the same building, they left Ruth alone but checked now and then to be sure she was all right.

Before the study was over, however, they heard a noise outside the apartment door and went into the hall to check. There at the foot of the stairs was little Ruth, with one hand high in the air as if holding someone's hand.

"How did you get down here?" they wanted to know.

And she said, "The angel brought me."[1]

Again, Ruth remembers nothing about this. She knows only what she was told. Any parent knows that small children sometimes have vivid imaginations, and for a three-year-old to negotiate stairs would not seem too unusual. However, this particular stairway, Ruth was told, was in total darkness and would have been dangerous for a child.

Did it happen? Or was it only a child's fantasy? I don't know. But one thing is certain. It is the sort of thing an angel would do if a child were in danger.

Angels, as they minister to us, are not doing a duty distasteful to them. They are not simply carrying out an assignment. Angels care too!

Angels record our prayers and our tears.[2] If we weep through discouragement, they cease to sing.[3] The first tear of repentance for sin creates joy among them.[4]

And listen to this: "The angels of glory find their joy in . . . giving love and tireless watchcare to souls that are fallen and unholy. Heavenly beings woo the hearts of men; they bring to this dark world light from the courts above; by gentle and patient ministry they move upon the human spirit, to bring the lost into a fellowship with Christ which is even closer than they themselves can know."[5]

Think of it! Angels work to bring us into a relationship with Christ that is even closer than they themselves can know! What unselfishness!

Why are angels so interested in us? "In this speck of a world, the heavenly universe manifests the greatest interest; for Jesus paid an infinite price for the souls of its inhabitants."[6]

Angels care because Jesus cared—cared enough to die for us. We are told that when the news of man's fall reached heaven, "angels were so interested for man's salvation that there could be found among them those who would yield their glory and give their life for perishing man." But "the transgression was so great that an angel's life would not pay the debt. Nothing but the death and intercession of God's Son would pay the debt and save lost man from hopeless sorrow and misery."[7]

Angels care too. Is it any wonder, then, that angels are kind? Is it any wonder that they delight in doing for us what we cannot do for ourselves—kind things, thoughtful things, needed things? Taking the hand of a little child in danger. Or filling the woodbox for a woman who could not fill it for herself.

It happened in a little cabin in Anchorage, Alaska, on a cold February morning. Mrs. Louise Dubay was alone and so badly crippled that she could not walk without applying hot-and-cold treatments to her leg. The cabin was heated by a wood-burning cookstove. She had many friends, but this morning for some reason no one had remembered to visit her and bring in a fresh supply of wood. And she couldn't call anyone, because she had no telephone at that time. In her desperation she began to pray aloud. Never before had she prayed so earnestly. But no one came.

Finally the last of the wood was gone, and the fire went out. It was thirty degrees below zero. The cabin began to chill rapidly, and she knew that, even protected as she was by blankets, she would soon freeze to death unless someone came and brought in wood for her. She kept praying, but no one came. And then she prayed a different kind of prayer. She told the Lord that if it was His will that she freeze to death, it was all right. She was willing.

About that time the door opened—the cabin had only one door—and in walked a tall young man carrying an armload of wood. He was not dressed as most people dress in Alaska during the winter months. He had on a black hat and a black overcoat. He put the wood in the woodbox and proceeded to make a fire in the stove. When the fire was burning well, he put water in the big teakettle and placed it over the fire.

All this time he seemed to keep his face turned so that she could not see his full face. He turned now and went out the door, returning shortly with another armload of firewood. She still had not really seen his face. Nor had he said a word.

Naturally Mrs. Dubay was awed by all this—so much so that she could not speak. She just sat there and looked at him, all the while wanting to ask him if he was an angel, yet afraid to speak up. Finally she asked him that question in her mind, without saying a word aloud. And when she did that, he turned toward her, smiled, and nodded his head. His face was so noble, she says, that she knew he was not from this world. He turned, opened the door, and left without saying a word.

For a time she just sat there, as if petrified. Finally she thought, "If he is an angel sent from God, there will not be any footprints in the snow outside the door." So she forced herself to hobble to the door, opened it, and looked out on the unruffled snow. There were no footprints. Neither had the snow been disturbed over, or around, her little pile of wood. The snow was perfectly smooth and rounded over as always after a snowstorm![8]

"In the heavenly school . . . every redeemed one will understand the ministry of angels in his own life. The angel who was his guardian from his earliest moment; the angel who watched his steps, and covered his head in the day of peril; the angel who was with him in the valley of the shadow of death, who marked his resting place, who was the first to greet him in the resurrection morning—what will it be to hold converse with him, and to learn the history of divine interposition in the individual life, of heavenly co-operation in every work for humanity!"[9]

I can hardly wait! Can you?

6—I.B.A.

Touching the Fringes

No book prepared by human hands could ever hold the full record of angel activity on behalf of fallen men. All around this planet these heavenly friends, twenty-four hours a day, are protecting, guiding, comforting, encouraging the adopted children of the King. Only occasionally are we privileged to see them. Silently, unobserved by human eyes, they note the prayers of repentant sinners and still-not-perfect saints. And then, directed by God, they use their incredible power to alter circumstances, to batter down mountains of difficulty—or to encourage and strengthen us in our waiting. Our prayers have been heard. But do we realize how often angels are involved?

It will take a fascinating piece of eternity to tell the full story of these celestial beings we seldom see. In these pages we can only touch the fringes. But now—a handful of nutshell accounts of what God does—with the assistance of the angels—when we pray.

Two-year-old Ray was lost in a cornfield. There was a river nearby—and a lake and a creek. It would soon be dark. Nearly twenty people had joined in the search but had found no trace of the little boy. His mother pleaded, "Help us, Lord! Help us find him before nightfall!"

Finally, helpless to know what else to do, his father dropped the reins on old Nellie's neck, grasped the saddle horn, and cried aloud, "O Lord, direct this horse to Ray!"

Instantly she started in a swift canter up along the creek bank. About a quarter of a mile to the north the creek made a loop, and here she started to leave the creek and follow a path across the field. Then the mare stopped dead still, as if an unseen hand had pulled on the reins. Nellie turned and walked straight into the thicket.

They were within twenty feet of Ray when his father saw him. But the horse didn't stop until she could have touched him. There he sat, calmly stripping leaves off a stock of switch cane. His little face was tear-stained, but he was unharmed. His father knelt beside him and offered a prayer of thanks. Then he put Ray on the saddle and swung up beside him. As the horse galloped, he called out, "Found! Found!" And the searchers relayed the happy news from one to another.

As his mother, overjoyed, pulled him from the saddle, he called out, "Mamma, big kitty! Pat big kitty!"

Many bobcats were found in southeast Missouri that year—1939. Could it be that the two-year-old boy had been in the company of a bobcat during those hours? His mother thought so. He talked about the big kitty for days.

Ray had a story he was too young to fill in. One day his guardian angel will tell what really happened![1]

Ruth Gibson, in the summer of 1977, was alone for a few days while her husband, Fred, attended a convention. She was a little nervous about being alone in the house at night, especially since a neighbor's home had just been burglarized. Also, the Gibsons had a broken window that had not yet been repaired. But the first evening she prayed, turned out all the lights, and went to bed about half-past eight.

The next morning her neighbor said to her, "Who was all the company last night?"

Ruth explained that she had had no company, that she had turned out all the lights and gone to bed early. And her neighbor said, "I looked over at your house several times last night, and it was all lit up. Looked like every light in the house was on. I thought you must have a lot of company."

Who turned on the lights? Was she in special danger? Did she have company she was not aware of? Were the house lights turned on at all? Or had her neighbor seen the light radiating from Ruth's angel protector? Someday she will know![2]

It was early in 1953 when a series of evangelistic meetings was in progress in Reno, Nevada. The presentation of Bible truth, as it sometimes does, aroused some opposition, and an evangelist from another state was called in to try to counteract the influence of our meetings.

One morning this visiting evangelist announced by radio that he would really expose Seventh-day Adventists at his meeting that evening. Two members of our evangelistic company attended the meeting. They arrived as some pictures were being shown. But almost immediately it was apparent that something was wrong, that something had happened to the pastor and the evangelist. When the evangelist stood up to speak, he seemed confused and ill. He simply read a few scriptures and sat down, never mentioning Seventh-day Adventists.

The next day it was learned that when our two men entered, the speakers on the platform recognized them. They and half the congregation saw not two men but six. The other four were burly men, and the

84

ministers were afraid of what might happen if Adventists were mentioned.

Strangely enough, the other half of the congregation saw only our two men. Many of those present that evening were convinced that angels of God had intervened, and twenty-two of them, by actual count, were present at our next meeting![3]

Opposition to truth is no problem for God. Nor does it take Him by surprise. Whatever the emergency, whatever the difficulty, He has a way prepared to meet it. And His timing is never wrong!

Jack Circle, then an assistant chaplain at one of our hospitals, was approached late one day by a businessman, a member of the church, who said he was in trouble. Jack said, "Let's go to my office and pray about it."

The businessman explained that he desperately needed money to meet his payroll. He would have the money in a week, but the payroll was coming up the next day. "How much do you need?" Jack asked. And he said, "I need $24,700." That was a lot of money to pray about. Jack gave him the telephone number of someone who might be able to help with a much smaller amount. But that didn't solve the problem.

Jack opened his Bible and read, "My God shall supply all your need." Philippians 4:19.

The two men knelt together and in faith claimed that promise. Then Jack had to leave for prayer meeting, and the businessman went home. He tried the number Jack had given him but received no answer. It seemed there was no way out of his dilemma. Then the telephone rang.

The call was from a friend in the northern part of the state. He said, "Thirty minutes ago I was impressed that you needed money." And the astonished man said, "Thirty minutes ago Jack Circle and I were kneeling in his office, claiming the promise, 'My God shall supply all your need.' "

The friend said he had sold some equipment for $21,700 and had $3000 in his safe. He would send the full amount immediately. Needless to say, the parties on both ends of that call were deeply impressed. The friend who called was a doctor. He was also an atheist! He said later, "Any God who uses me to answer a prayer, I want to know."[4]

Would it be wrong to suggest that God and His angels must have fun working out our problems in such refreshingly unexpected ways?

Pine Springs Ranch was running out of water. Two hundred juniors had used a lot of water. Family camp, now in progress, was using much less. But the tanks, supplied by nearby mountain wells, were not filling up. They were almost empty. If it did not rain very, very soon, the camp would have to close after a season of only two weeks.

Those present at family camp prayed earnestly for rain. The next day clouds gathered and a few drops fell—not enough to change the situation at all.

Friday evening after campfire the campers gathered for prayer again. Why had not God answered their prayers? Should they be more specific? Should they set a time limit? Should they ask God to send rain by Monday morning? Would that be faith or presumption? They decided they should not tell God how to answer their prayers but simply leave the matter in His hands. In that spirit they prayed.

As soon as they rose from their knees, some ran to check the tanks, as they had been doing every few hours. The others were saying good night to each other. Suddenly a shout rang out over the camp, "Water! There is water in the tanks!"

Now those last to leave the prayer circle raced to the

tanks. Even as they ran, they could hear the sound of flowing water. Someone shouted, "The tanks are full and running over!"

Five hours earlier those tanks were empty. Now they were full and running over.[5]

Evidently rain is not the only way God can fill water tanks!

The Seventh-day Adventist elementary school in Vacaville, California, had just been remodeled. That is, it had been remodeled except for shingles. Funds had run just that much short. And the need was serious, for the rainy season was approaching.

The smaller children, in Kay Buzelli's room, had memorized the words of Jesus, "With men this is impossible; but with God all things are possible." And they believed those words were true. For days they had prayed for shingles. And earlier that September morning, in Bible class, Karen had prayed, "Dear Jesus, please be with us today. Help us to do something to show we love others. And please, dear God, don't forget to take care of our school."

And then it happened. The freeway was only a stone's throw away. And suddenly there was a great "boom" as a giant truck tire blew out. Seventeen frightened children looked up to see the big truck swerve into the path of oncoming traffic. But those little people, believe it or not, did not race outside, or even to the window, to see what was happening. One of them said, "Let's pray that no one will be hurt." And seventeen children knelt in a circle with their teacher and prayed—while the screeching, thumping, bumping, crashing sounds of a serious accident continued.

Their prayer was answered even as they prayed. The big truck had turned over and dumped its contents on the edge of the freeway. A smaller truck, in which a two-year-old boy was riding with his father, had turned over and landed in the creek beside the school. But there were no serious injuries. Even the newspapers called it a miracle.

But wait! What had the big truck dumped on the edge of the freeway? Shingles! Shingles just the color needed for the school! Shingles strewn everywhere, it seemed! And nobody wanted to pick them up!

A school board member was at the school at the time, and he negotiated with the insurance adjuster to buy them all for a very small sum. The children picked them up and stacked them neatly. The roof was cared for before the rains, and the shingles left over were sold for a profit of $300![6]

Could anyone tell those Vacaville children that God doesn't answer prayer?

Dave and his wife, Grace, were awakened in the middle of the night by the sound of the doorbell. Who could it be? Dave made his way down to the front door. There was no one there. Looking up and down the street, he saw a man standing in front of the neighbor's house, looking back at him. Then the man walked down the street and disappeared.

The next night at three o'clock the doorbell rang again. Dave was more cautious this time. He left the night chain latched and just cracked the door. "Who is there?" And a male voice answered, "I'm looking for John Smith. Does he live here?" And Dave said, "No, I'm sorry. He doesn't live here. Good night." He didn't know if it was the same person as the night before, but of course he suspected that it was.

For several nights neither Dave nor Grace slept well. Their collie dog, kept in the backyard, barked more than usual. Once Dave looked out and saw a man dressed like the one he had seen the first night.

Five or six uneasy nights passed, and they were getting more jumpy with each succeeding night.

Friday morning they discovered that a window had been broken out during the night. All the first-floor windows had bars; but blinds on this window, coming between the bars and the windowpane, would have prevented a prowler from seeing the bars.

Concern now showed on their faces as they hurried the children off to school.

Dave picked the children up that afternoon. As he turned into the driveway, he saw a man, dressed like the one he had seen, walking toward their house. He let the children out and told them to go into the house immediately. Then he walked around to the front to confront the man. But the man had seen him and was now five or six houses down the street.

What could he do? He had no proof it was the same man. What could he be arrested for? Dave, not wanting to alarm Grace, told her he had a few more visits to make and would be back in an hour.

About thirty minutes later Grace heard the back door open and someone come in. She thought Dave had forgotten something and went to see if she could help. To her horror she was standing face-to-face with a strange man. He said, "Hi, how are y'all?" but stopped where he was. Grace, exhibiting a cool she did not feel, said, "I'm just fine." Then she walked deliberately toward him. Taken by surprise, he backed out the door, and she locked it. She was in a state of near panic.

But what could Dave and Grace do? The man was gone now, and probably many men dressed in a black hat and black topcoat. That evening, after the children were in bed, they prayed earnestly that angels would protect them all.

The collie dog barked again that night. Dave saw the same man walking away. Then everything was quiet.

Sabbath morning they awoke a little late, having lost so much sleep. Instantly Grace said, "Dave, I smell cigarette smoke! Someone has been in this house!" Dave smelled it too and investigated. Someone *had* been in the house. Someone was *still there*— lying on the stairs. Dave called the police, "We have an intruder in our house. He's lying on the stairs. I don't know if he's drunk, asleep, sick, or dead. But please hurry!"

Nervously they waited. What would happen now? Would the man come upstairs? Was he dead? The minutes seemed like hours. When the patrol car drove up, Dave opened the door for the officer. "There's the man lying up there on the stairway. He must be either drunk or drugged to go to sleep on the stairs like that."

The officer pointed his flashlight at the man. "That man is not asleep. He's wide awake!" Then to the man, "This is the police. Stand up! Put your hands behind your back!"

He stood up, was handcuffed, and taken away.

The man confessed that he had been staking out the house for about two months. He wouldn't say why. He said he had been upstairs, looking into the bedrooms, when he heard Dave and Grace begin to wake up. He started down the stairs and then, for some reason he didn't know, he lay down on the stairs and stayed there until the officer told him to get up.

Police were amazed. They couldn't understand. But Dave and Grace and the children do not think it so strange. They believe that the Lord commanded him to lie down and that the angels kept him there until the officer arrived![7]

That account was more than a nutshell, wasn't it?

There is the story of Jim, who, without realizing it, carried a pocket calculator he had been looking at out of a store, along with his purchases. When he got to the car, he tossed his packages onto the front seat and one of them slid to the floor. As he bent over to pick it up, he saw the calculator underneath it. To anyone looking on, of course, it would appear that he was trying to hide it.

And someone *was* looking on. Just at that moment the store owner opened the car door and demanded that he get out. He was arrested for shoplifting.

This was a serious blow. Jim and his family were new in the city. Nobody knew him. His job and his reputation were at stake. It was the next day before he could get up courage to tell Janine what had happened. "It was so stupid," he said, "so stupid!" He felt he had to plead guilty. After all, the calculator was in his possession when he was arrested. No one would be concerned about whether he *meant* to take it or not.

He was called before the judge the next Friday, and the charges were read. There were the usual formalities. But when the judge asked if he had anything to say, he explained what had happened. The judge interrupted. "Just a minute. Are you trying to say that you did not *intend* to take this calculator?"

"No, I did not, Your Honor."

"Then I can't accept your plea of guilty. This case will have to be held over for trial in a criminal court." The trial was set for November 20.

Jim and Janine were praying constantly these days—praying as they had never prayed before.

The trial was on a Thursday. Six witnesses testified against Jim. Then his lawyer called for a recess and told Jim he could get him off on a technicality. None of the witnesses could prove it was the same calculator. Jim didn't want that. And then the judge had to leave to catch a plane. Court was adjourned until the next Tuesday.

Jim and Janine kept praying. Janine fasted one day.

All that mattered was that she must be right with God. Otherwise, how could He hear her prayers? Then she experienced a calm and a peace she had not known before.

On Tuesday all the judge had to do was sum up his findings and give his verdict. But something was added. The judge had a story to tell of what had happened to him on Saturday. Shopping in the Redlands Shopping Center, he made several purchases and looked at a number of other items. As he was getting into his car, he suddenly realized he had accidentally picked up an item and brought it out with him. "If I had been stopped then," he told the lawyers, "I would have been in exactly the same predicament as this man."

And then, "Not guilty. Case dismissed."[8]

Angels must have wept tears of joy along with Jim and Janine!

But I must tell you one more. Three little girls, and three little girls who were visiting them, suddenly decided they wanted to get the Shetland pony and take turns riding.

There was no reason they shouldn't ride, except that the pony was out in the south pasture, running with some yearling steers. And this particular pony loved her freedom. She could run faster than most Shetlands, and she knew every trick of escape. It took two well-mounted men to bring her in.

The father who owned the horse explained to the girls that he couldn't bring her in alone, and he tried to suggest something else they might do. But after a hurried conference the six little girls just dropped to their knees and began to pray. The problem, to them, was so simple. God could bring the pony in.

It was a sight to remember—six little girls with their heads together, praying so earnestly. The father was almost moved to join them. But he wondered if it might not be a sacrilege to pray for a range-running horse to come home. And it seemed so futile.

He was about to tell them that one doesn't ask God for such things, when he looked up and saw the pony coming on the run—down the butte, across the flat, through the creek, and into the corral, where she stopped and waited. The girls by now were up from their knees and waiting for her. They weren't even surprised. They just ran for her with cries of joy, got her bridled, and took her off for an afternoon of riding.

The father of the visiting girls was absolutely shaken. His face was white. He said to his host, "It seems it's not what you pray for but who does the praying!"

He had just seen six little girls blast every rule of horsemanship. He wouldn't have believed the story if it had been told him. But he had seen it and couldn't forget. He began reading his Bible and then attending church with his family. He has since held several offices in the church. Before witnessing what happened that day, religion had meant nothing to him. His faith is now unshakable![9]

Could the same be said of *your* faith—now? If not, why?

The Wonder of Commitment

Why is it that some people live a humdrum existence, perpetually on the brink of despair—while others, fascinated by the artistry of each new sunset, delighted by the song of the birds, live forever on the edge of wonder?

Why is it that some dreary souls are always expecting the worst—while others are busy thanking God for miracles that haven't happened yet?

Drudgery will blow out a man's hope, if he lets it. But wonder walks on tiptoe, ready for anything!

Stories of God's power and of the loving care of angels ought to boost our faith to a new high. But in the reaction of some of you there may be a hint of discouragement. Someone may be saying, "Why do all the spectacular things happen to other people? I pray. I've prayed all my life. But nothing extraordinary happens to me. Why?"

And that's a good question to ask. Because it ought not to be that way. It doesn't need to be.

It is possible that some of us have never experienced a spectacular deliverance from danger simply because we have never been in that kind of danger. God does not work miracles for show. He works where there is a need.

But the problem goes deeper than that. Answers to prayer—just as definite, though not necessarily as spectacular—ought to be an everyday thing in the life of the Christian. If it isn't that way, there has to be a reason!

Have you ever tried demonstrating the faith you say you have by thanking God for things He does before He does them? I'm not advocating presumption. Certainly I'm not suggesting that we *demand* anything of God, or set time limits for Him, or tell Him how to answer our prayers, or even ask for some sign that He hears us. Every request we make must be left in His hands, to be answered according to His will, with a negative answer just as acceptable to us as an affirmative one.

As for a sign that He hears us, why should we need it? *The evidence is in the promise!*

We know the Bible definition of faith. "Faith is the substance of things hoped for, the evidence of things not seen." Hebrews 11:1.

Substance. That's pretty real, isn't it, pretty substantial. That's something to take hold of. Now tell me, If you have the substance of what you hope for, if you actually have it, what is the first thing you do? You thank God for it, don't you? So faith thanks God, thanks Him enthusiastically—even though it cannot yet *see* the thing it hopes for. Faith knows it has the answer. *The evidence is in the promise!*

Now this may seem like going out on a limb. It may seem almost insane to tell people God is going to sell your house at just the right time—when you haven't had a nibble for six months. But faith can thank Him every day—and with real enthusiasm—that He is going to do just that. This doesn't mean He will do it on any certain day, or sell it to the person you have picked out, or for the exact price you have in mind. It just means He will take care of the matter in the best way—in His way and in His time. And besides, if He doesn't want you to sell it at all, do you want to?

I might as well confess that I had this very experience recently. Not a nibble for more than six months. But I kept telling people that God would sell it at the right time. And I kept thanking Him. Actually, if the house had sold during those months, it would have been a serious problem, for I had no place to move. But five days after circumstances were such that I could move, three couples wanted the house!

In this matter of thanking God for what He does before He does it, I am not taking an extreme position. The servant of the Lord says, "Not because we see or feel that God hears us, are we to believe. We are to trust in His promises. When we come to Him in faith, every petition enters the heart of God. When we have asked for His blessing, we should believe that we receive it, and thank Him that we *have* received it. Then we are to go about our duties, assured that the blessing will be realized when we need it most. When we have learned to do this, we shall know that our prayers are answered. God will do for us 'exceeding abundantly,' 'according to the riches of His glory,' and 'the working of His mighty power.' "[1]

Catch the highlights of this marvelous statement. "Not because we see." "Thank Him that we *have* received it." And then this priceless sentence: "When we have learned to do this, we shall know that our prayers are answered."

Are you learning? Do you know how to take a request to God and get an answer?

It was many years ago that the manager of one of our large sanitariums was invited to accept the supervision of another, larger institution. He was reluctant to go, especially because his children were attending a nearby college. Yet he wanted to do the Lord's will. Finally he asked counsel of W. C. White, son of Ellen White, who had long been a friend. And W. C. White was surprised by the question. He placed his hand on the younger man's shoulder and asked, "Do you mean to tell me, Myron, that after all these years in the Lord's work, you haven't learned how to get down on your knees, ask God a question, and get an answer?"[2]

The pen of inspiration tells us how: "Those who decide to do nothing in any line that will displease God, will know, after presenting their case before Him, just what course to pursue. And they will receive not only wisdom, but strength. Power for obedience, for service, will be imparted to them, as Christ has promised."[3]

Those who can go to their knees and get an answer are those who have made a very special commitment to their Lord. "Those who decide to do nothing in any line that will displease God" are those who have made a complete commitment, an unreserved commitment, an unreserved surrender to His will. There can be no barrier, nothing held back, no idols, no other gods.

What have we done with Jesus? That is the question. Lloyd John Ogilvie says it so well: "Take him in! Accept him as the greatest man who ever lived! Revere him as the most penetrating psychologist who ever analyzed life. Mark the calendar B. C. and A. D. Plan your customs around his birth, death, and resurrection. Speak of the gentle Jesus, meek and mild. Paint portraits of him, write the libraries full of line and verse about him. Sing for him; preach about him. We will have done everything we can with human skill and adoration—except one—made him the absolute Lord of our lives!"[4]

Everything except make Him Lord. But nothing else will do!

97

If your prayer experience, or mine, is humdrum, there has to be a reason. For there is no limit to what the Lord Jesus will do for us if we will not hold Him at a distance. But if we would live on the edge of wonder, we must leave our gods behind. For *heaven begins when we let go of earth!*

What happens to our prayers depends upon the quality of our relationship with the Lord Jesus. If that relationship is casual, our experience will be casual. God does not want a halfhearted commitment. He wants all there is of us. Yet we shrink from that kind of commitment. We hold back from a complete surrender.

But the man who doesn't want to get into Christianity too deep, the man who wants to keep a hand on the parachute so he can jump out if he chooses—that man is left holding a hollow profession that can never satisfy. He will never know what might have been!

The way to miss it all is to go only halfway. If we stop short of complete surrender, we find the Christian life only an intolerable burden. We miss the wonder and excitement that Jesus has planned for us. Heaven is so near we can almost touch it. But it is *only for those who have let go of earth!*

The wonder of a fully surrendered life cannot be described. It can only be experienced. The excitement of answered prayer. The companionship of angels. Days so filled with happy surprises that you can hardly wait for tomorrow to see what God is up to next!

Faith grows fast when you live constantly on the edge of wonder. Ceilings are soon gone. Horizons are pushed back. There is no limit to what God can do for and with the man or woman or youth who makes an unreserved commitment. When such a one runs out of earth, heaven is waiting!

The Clock That Struck Thirteen

Some stories are so outstanding that they deserve a separate telling. This is the first of four favorites of mine that belong in that category. Or so it seems to me.

It was midnight in the town of Plymouth, England. Two men stood by the town's great clock. As it finished striking the hour, both men, strangers, remarked that it had struck thirteen times instead of twelve. One of these men was a gentleman by the name of Captain Jarvis.

It was not long after this that Captain Jarvis awoke early one morning, got up, dressed, and went down to the front door of his home. As he opened it, he saw, to his surprise, that his groom was standing there, with his horse saddled and bridled, ready for him to mount.

The groom explained, "I had a feeling that you would be wanting your horse, sir." He said the feeling had been so strong that he couldn't stay in bed but had to get up and get the horse ready.

This was strange. It had never happened before. But since the horse was ready, he mounted and rode off. Not having to go anywhere in particular, he let the horse choose where he would take him. Soon they were down by the river, close to the spot where a ferry took passengers across.

Imagine his surprise, at this early hour, to see the ferryman there with his boat, waiting to take him across. What was going on?

"How are you here so early, my man?" he inquired.

"I couldn't rest in my bed, sir, for I had a feeling I was wanted to ferry someone across."

The captain and the horse got on the boat, and soon they were on the other side. Now what? Again he let the horse direct the course he would take. After some time they came to a large country town. And seeing a passerby, the captain inquired if anything of interest was going on in the town.

"No, sir. Nothing but the trial of a man for murder."

So, with no other destination in mind for this strange trip, he thought he would see what was going on. He rode to the place of the trial, dismounted, and entered the building.

As he walked in, he heard the judge saying to the prisoner, "Have you anything to say for yourself—anything at all?"

And the prisoner said, "I have nothing to say, sir, except that I am an innocent man. There is only one man in all the world who could prove my innocence, but I do not know his name nor where he lives. Some weeks ago we stood together in the town of Plymouth when it was midnight. We both heard the great town clock strike thirteen instead of twelve, and we remarked about it to each other—how strange it was that the clock should strike thirteen at the midnight hour."

"I am here! I am here!" the captain shouted from the rear of the room. "I was the man who stood at midnight beside the great Plymouth clock and heard it strike thirteen instead of twelve. What the prisoner says is absolutely true. I identify him as the man. On the night of the murder, at the very time it was committed, that man was with me at Plymouth, and we remarked to each other how strange it was that the clock should strike thirteen at the midnight hour!"

The condemned man, proved innocent by the captain's testimony, was immediately set free![1]

Think of it! Only one man in the world could prove that prisoner's innocence. And angels, by awakening a groom and a ferryman and impressing them with an urgency they could not understand—and by leading the horse—had brought that one man into the courtroom at the precise moment he was needed!

How the angels must have loved it!

The Bushman's Story

In the remote sandy wastes of the Kalahari Desert—in Bechuanaland, now known as Botswana, southern Africa—lived the primitive Bushmen. They had never known civilization. They lived where the white man seldom went and never stayed. Sekuba, a Bushman, was fully grown but only five feet tall.

When Sekuba and his family crept in out of the desert cold one night in 1953, they had no inkling that their way of life was about to change forever. Sekuba kept his bow and his quiver of poisoned arrows near him.

The Bushmen knew nature and knew her secrets. They knew where to find the roots that yielded the poison for their arrowheads. They knew where to find the shells of wild ostrich eggs that they could fill with water when it rained briefly. They knew the forbidden desert. They had survived incredible hardship. But generations of their way of life seemed to have almost effaced the image of their Creator.

Sekuba's family slept. But for him the night was suddenly brighter than day, and he talked with one who spoke from the fire he saw!

The next morning he tried to tell his wife and family what had happened. Over and over he tried. They attached great significance to dreams, but who had ever heard of a dream like this? What was the Book he was talking about? And who was the shining one who had spoken from the fire, so bright he could not look at him? Why must Sekuba go to the east to find the people who had the Book and could tell him about God? Why did he feel he must leave this very day because of the angel's command? They couldn't comprehend it.

"How will you speak to the people you will meet?" they wanted to know. The Bushmen spoke a language of clicks and gutteral sounds not at all like the languages spoken by Bantu natives. No one would ever go to the Bushmen with books. Their language had never been reduced to writing. It was seldom that Bantus or whites ventured near them, for with their poison arrows shot from ambush they were to be feared.

But Sekuba told his family, "The Book talks. The shining one taught me the words of the Book. I understood them, and I will be able to read them."

His family made no attempt to remind him of the dangers he would find along the way. They were impressed, too, by his night vision—impressed enough to travel with him a part of the way.

Each day they drew nearer the eastern border of Bechuanaland, hunting to sustain themselves. Finally, on the fringe of civilization, they found some scattered Bushmen who knew a little more about their Bantu neighbors. Sekuba left his family near them, and they believed his promise to return when he had found the people with the Book.

Clad in his skin loincloth, carrying his blanket made of animal hide and a scanty supply of dried meat, armed with his bow and poison-tipped arrows, he advanced eastward alone into the unknown, as the angel had directed.

103

Many days later, a hundred and fifty miles from his original starting place, Sekuba hesitantly approached the huts of some African Bantu farmers. The tribesman at the first hut was startled and not a little frightened to see a Bushman standing before him. But he saw that the bow in his hand was empty; so he did not flee. Sekuba waited respectfully for him to speak.

"I see you," said the Bantu, according to African custom.

With dignity Sekuba returned the greeting and then asked, "Where will I find the people with the Book?" The amazed Bantu could find no words for a moment, and Sekuba continued, "I have come to find the people who worship God."

"You speak our language!" the African burst out.

"The shining one taught me," Sekuba said simply, and then he told more about his night vision. "Can you take me to one who can teach me more of the Book?"

"This is marvelous," exclaimed the Bantu. "Yes, I can take you to our pastor. He lives near."

They started out together, their progress impeded by excited Bantus who crowded around, wanting to see this Bushman who had been taught to speak the Tswana language by a supernatural being. It was near dusk when the group—it was a group now, for others had joined the two along the way—reached the humble dwelling that had real windows with glass panes. They told their excited story, and then the pastor wanted to hear it direct from Sekuba.

The little Bushman was not awed by his strange surroundings. Rather, he was happy for the success of his mission and glad to tell of the vision that was responsible for his long journey. When he had finished, he asked humbly, "Have I found the people who worship God—and have the Book?"

The pastor, deeply moved, entered his house and

returned with a Bible in his hand. Sekuba's eyes lighted up. He clapped his hands softly and bowed his head as he exclaimed, "That is it! That is the Book!"

"This is the end of your journey!" the pastor exclaimed. "You shall stay with me tonight." He led the group in prayer, and the Africans returned to their huts. Sekuba was made comfortable in the little hut that served as the pastor's kitchen. A servant prepared food for him. Then he lay down to sleep, happy to have found the object of his search.

But that night the angel came again. "This is not the true church," the shining one said. "You must continue your search. You must find the Sabbath-keeping church and ask for Pastor Moyo. He will not only have the Book but also four brown books that are really nine."

So in the morning Sekuba explained to his host, "I must leave you. I cannot stay here. The shining one came in the night and told me to find a people who keep the seventh day as Sabbath."

The pastor could not believe his ears. "This is the chief's church," he said, with irritation in his voice. "Would the chief be wrong? You have not understood."

Sekuba was respectful, but he was also firm. "Sir, I have not misunderstood. These things were shown me plainly. There are people who worship God on the seventh day. Please tell me where I may find them."

Now there was anger. A crowd gathered. Sekuba was arrested for defying the chief's church. But he never changed his story. Finally he was set free by the white commissioner, who felt something akin to awe as he saw an unlearned Bushman speaking Tswana and holding firmly to his story of angel instruction.

Safely on his way again, Sekuba spent the night where darkness found him. But he was troubled. How could he find Pastor Moyo? What direction should he take? Alone in the desert he talked with the unseen God and asked Him to direct him, to give him some sign. Then he fell asleep.

In the light of dawn he saw near the distant horizon a small, mistlike cloud. That, in the clear dry air bordering the desert, he accepted as his sign. Patiently he followed it. For seven days and 118 miles it led him on. Carefully he avoided roads and men, for one mistake was enough.

Somewhere—it may have been before he left the shelter of the commissioner's court—he had acquired some European clothes. So now he did not look so conspicuous as he entered a little settlement. The cloud that had gone before him now disappeared. Would he be able to find Pastor Moyo?

The next morning a Bantu African directed him into the village, and he had no difficulty in finding Pastor Moyo's home. The pastor was startled at the sight of his visitor. Like other Africans, he harbored some fear of Bushmen. But as he studied his face, he knew that this was no ordinary African, and he invited him in.

Once again Sekuba told his story in Tswana while the pastor listened with growing awe and wonder. And the little Bushman said, as he finished his story, "I am commanded to find the people with the Book who keep the seventh-day Sabbath."

Gladly Pastor Moyo brought out his worn Bible and assured him that he had found the people he was looking for.

"That is it!" Sekuba exclaimed. But he had one more request. "Where are the four books that are really nine?"

Pastor Moyo turned to his bookshelf and brought out the four brown volumes bearing the title *Testimonies for the Church.*

Every Seventh-day Adventist is familiar with these books from the pen of Ellen White, whose writing bears the marks and meets every test of inspiration—nine volumes, at one time bound for convenience into four books.

Sekuba was satisfied and delighted. He said eagerly, "You are the people!"

His journey was ended. But there was so much more—so much more to learn. All that day they talked and read from the Book. For two weeks they studied together, and Sekuba drank it all in.

Then Sekuba returned to his own people with the good news about Jesus, and Pastor Moyo visited them. It was discovered that the Bushmen, even with their primitive background, had phenomenal memories. They were able to memorize long passages of Scripture in a short time without forgetting them.

Sekuba became church elder, evangelist, and pastor of the first Bushman church. And he retained until his death in 1957 the ability to speak, read, and write the Tswana language—the ability given him by the shining one who spoke to him from the fire.![1]

You and I need make no long, tiring, dangerous journey to find the Book. By comparison, the light that floods our path is blinding. Do we follow it as carefully, as persistently, as did the little man from the African bush?

Only One Key

Sundar Singh. It was he whose little world collapsed when his mother died as he was near fourteen. Despondent, dejected, he was angry at God and angry at the world. In his despair he bought a copy of the Christian's Bible so that he could tear it page by page and throw it on the fire.

Then, in deep gloom, he retired to his room and stayed there for days. One night he prayed earnestly, "Oh, God—if there be a God—reveal Thyself to me tonight." The express from Ludhiana to Lahore would go by at five in the morning, and he determined that if God had not revealed Himself by then, he would go out and lay his head on the rails and settle the matter. He prayed on through the night.

At a quarter to five he rushed out of his room and awakened his father. He told him he had seen a vision of Jesus and was now a Christian!

His father said, "You must be mad! You come while I am sleeping and say you are a Christian—and yet it is not three days past that you burned the Christian book!"

Sundar stood rigid, looking at his hands. "These hands did it. I can never cleanse them of that sin till the day I die!" Then he turned to his father. "But till that day comes my life is His!"

And that's the way it was. Because he wanted to win India for Christ and because there was much prejudice against all things Western, he adopted the yellow robe of the sadhu and wore it till his death.

Sadhu Sundar Singh had a great burden, too, for Tibet. And he was a born adventurer. Almost every summer, the rest of his life, he managed somehow to get into Tibet. And the more he was persecuted, the happier he was.

One summer things had gone especially bad. From the day he crossed the mountains there was trouble. Villagers refused him any hospitality. He nearly drowned in a swift-flowing, icy river. Food was scarce. He was cruelly treated. Lamas and priests led the peasants in their persecution of him. Preaching Jesus in Tibet could easily mean death. But death held few terrors for him. He was concerned only with being true to his Lord.

Matters reached a climax in a town called Razar. He began preaching in the marketplace, sleeping at night in the unsheltered compound where traders and beasts pressed together for warmth. At first his preaching drew interested crowds. But when the chief lama heard of his preaching, the interest of the people changed to fury.

One morning the guard from the monastery seized the sadhu and dragged him away to a brief trial. And as he looked into the hard face of the Grand Lama, he knew that one of two things would happen to him. He would either be sewn inside a wet yak skin and it would be left in the heat of the sun to dry and shrink until it crushed him to death; or he would be thrown into a deep, dry well on top of the corpses of those who had been thrown there before him, to die of starvation.

It was the well. He was dragged there and beaten

and thrashed until a blow sent him headlong into it. Then he heard the lid being locked. The stench was sickening, for many others had died there.

Sundar prayed for deliverance, but how it could come he had no idea. One of his arms was broken; so he could not possibly climb to the top. Even if he could, he could not get out, for the Grand Lama himself had the only key, and by now it would be jangling again on the key ring under his robes.

Hours passed and became days. Three days and nights he had spent in the unbearable air of the well. And then suddenly he heard a key turn in the lock. The lid opened, creaking on its rusty hinge. Then he felt a rope touch his face. At the end of the rope was a loop. He thrust his leg into the loop and grasped the rope with his good arm. Slowly he was drawn upward to the top, where he collapsed on the ground and filled his lungs with the fresh night air. But when he looked around, his deliverer had disappeared!

Slowly and painfully he crawled back to the place where he had slept before. Snatches of sleep refreshed him. When it was light, he bathed, ridding himself of the smell of death—and went back to the marketplace to preach!

An hour later he was arrested again by furious monks. The Grand Lama questioned him over and over again. Who had helped him escape? Was it a man or a woman? And whoever it was, how did he or she get the key? That was the big question. There was only one key, and it should be in the Lama's possession. The Lama pulled aside his robes, stood up, and drew the bunch of keys from the chain.

"There is but one key to the well. It should be *here*. Who stole it to set you free? How . . ." Suddenly his features took on a look of terror. He turned to the monks, furious and inwardly afraid. "Take this man

110

away . . . away from the town. . . . Set him free . . . and never let him set foot again in Razar!"

The key to the well was on his own ring!

Sundar trusted God for everything—for protection, for food, for whatever he needed. And when asked about his seeming immunity from danger, he said simply that God protected him. And evidently God did. For even wild animals did not harm him.

On one occasion he was staying in the home of a friend in the Simla Hills. Supper was over, and the two sat quietly on the veranda. When there was a break in the conversation, Sundar moved away, slipping across the lawn toward the forest trees that bounded the garden. He stood there, gazing at the lights of villages across the valley.

Suddenly his friend, still on the veranda, tensed and rose to his feet, terrified at what he saw. Creeping slowly out of the trees came a leopard. It paused, gazed for a moment at the motionless sadhu, and then moved toward him. The friend dared not shout, for fear of causing the animal to spring. But he couldn't be silent either.

Quietly Sundar turned, saw the animal, and stretched out his hand toward it. The leopard rose, moved forward, and stood beside Sundar, who stroked its head as he would a pet animal. The watcher relaxed. There was no need to fear. There never had been. The leopard stood, lifting its head to Sundar now and then. And when the sadhu turned to the house, the leopard's powerful form disappeared among the trees. [1]

Is it too much to believe that the angels who released Peter from prison and who shut the mouths of lions for Daniel could do the same for Sundar Singh?

Or for you?

The Thunder at Eight

A father and his son farmed a small piece of land. Several times a year they would load up the oxcart with vegetables and drive to the nearest city.

The two had little in common. The son was the go-getter type. But the father believed in taking time to enjoy life.

One morning they loaded the cart, hitched up the ox, and set out. The son figured that if they kept going all day and all night, they could be in the city the next morning. He kept prodding the ox with a stick.

But the father said, "Take it easy. You'll last longer."

"But if we get to market ahead of the others, we have a better chance of getting good prices."

Four hours down the road they came to a little house. "Here's your uncle's place," said the father. "Let's stop in and say hello."

"We've lost an hour already," complained the go-getter.

"Then a few minutes more won't matter. My brother and I live so close and see each other so seldom."

So the young man fidgeted while the two old gentlemen gossiped away an hour.

On their way again, they came to a fork in the road,

and the old man directed the ox to the right.

"The left is shorter," said the boy.

"I know it, but this way is prettier."

The young man was impatient. "Have you no respect for time?"

"I respect it very much. That's why I like to use it for looking at pretty things."

The way led through a woodland with wild flowers. But the young man was busy watching the sun slip away. All he could think of was the time they had lost. He didn't even notice the flowers or the beautiful sunset.

Twilight found them in what looked like one big garden. And the old man said, "Let's sleep here."

The boy was really angry now. "This is the last trip I take with you! You're more interested in flowers than in making money."

The father only smiled. "That's the nicest thing you've said in a long time." Soon they were asleep.

A little before sunrise, the young man shook his father awake. They hitched up the ox and went on. But a mile down the road they came upon a farmer trying to pull his cart out of a ditch. "Let's give him a hand," said the father.

And the son exploded, "And lose more time?"

"Relax," said the old man. "You might be in a ditch yourself sometime."

It was almost eight o'clock when they got the other cart back on the road. Suddenly a great flash of lightning split the sky. Then there was thunder. The sky grew dark beyond the hills. "Looks like a big rain in the city."

And the son grumbled, "If we had been on time, we'd be sold out by now."

"Take it easy," said the old gentleman. "You'll last longer."

113

It was late afternoon when they reached the top of the hill overlooking the city. They stood for a long time looking down. Neither said a word. Finally the young man broke the silence. "I see what you mean, Father."

They turned their cart around and drove away from what had been, until eight o'clock that morning, the city of Hiroshima![1]

Credentials, Please

It had been the usual Christmas-day rush, and June was dead tired. But company had gone now, dishes were done, and she could unwind.

June's mother, however, was staying over for a time. Her mother was an agnostic—not antagonistic to Christianity but definitely not a believer.

June said, "Mom, I'll take you down to Christmas Tree Lane after a while, but I just have to rest a few minutes." Soon she fell asleep.

June was a very sound sleeper. The next thing she knew, a voice seemed to shake her awake. "Get up! Your mother is trying to kill herself!"

The voice was so urgent that June stood up instantly. But she was bewildered. She was not aware that her mother was depressed at all, and she simply refused to believe what the voice had said. Certain that her mother was just resting in her bedroom, she tapped lightly on the closed door and called. A voice from inside, sounding like someone almost asleep, answered, "What?"

Here was the proof, she thought, that her mother was all right. Yet there was something not quite right about the voice from the bedroom. She opened the door, only to find the room empty!

Now she was frightened. But she still couldn't believe that her mother was trying to take her own life. Then the voice that spoke to her originally said, "She's in the garage with the motor running!"

June walked into the kitchen, still hesitating. And the voice said, "You'd better hurry, or it will be too late!"

At that she rushed to the garage and found her mother already unconscious. When she revived she was unhappy at first that her suicide attempt had not succeeded. But June was able to convince her that her life had been spared for a purpose. Several years later she accepted Christ and was baptized.[1]

Here is an unusual incident, involving as it does two different voices. June believes that the voice from the bedroom was that of an evil angel who wanted her mother to die without making her decision for Christ. It illustrates well the determination of evil angels both to deceive and to destroy.

With so many instances of angel intervention fresh in our minds, it would be easy to forget that *not all angels* are spending their time in helping and protecting us. It would be easy to forget that there is a war on—a controversy between Christ and Satan that is fast escalating to its final climax. And angels are involved—two kinds of angels!

"And there was war in heaven. Michael and his angels fought against the dragon, and the dragon and his angels fought back. But he was not strong enough, and they lost their place in heaven. The great dragon was hurled down—that ancient serpent called the devil or Satan, who leads the whole world astray. He was hurled to the earth, and his angels with him." Revelation 12:7-9, N.I.V.

What does this mean to us? It means that in the invisible world about us there are billions of loyal angels assigned to help and protect us—and billions of rebel angels, fallen angels, angels turned demons, who are dead set to destroy us if they can!

So how can you tell one from the other? If you should meet an angel, how could you know whether he is a loyal angel or a rebel angel, a good angel or a bad angel? How could you know whether or not to believe what he tells you? By his appearance? Certainly not. For the apostle Paul says, "Satan himself masquerades as an angel of light. It is not surprising, then, if his servants masquerade as servants of righteousness." 2 Corinthians 11:14, 15, N.I.V.

So a being appearing as an angel of light may be only a masquerading demon trying to deceive you. How are you going to keep from being fooled?

Keep in mind that angels, both kinds of angels, also appear in human form. And angels, both kinds, can work miracles. Both are supernatural. Both are highly intelligent. Bad angels can do everything that good angels can—except that God places certain restrictions on the rebel angels.

"For they are the spirits of devils, working miracles." Revelation 16:14.

Fallen angels can work miracles too. So if a being, with or without wings, looking like an angel or looking like a man, does something supernatural, works a miracle, it doesn't necessarily mean that one of God's angels is around. Jumping effortlessly over a wall, or suddenly disappearing, or leaving no tracks, or having perfectly clean shoes after walking through the mud, or being surrounded by a brilliant light, or telling you something that no human being could know—none of these things means that his credentials are necessarily in order!

Does this mean, then, that we are simply at the mercy of these rebel angels that are all around us? No, it doesn't. God has given us a test, a way to identify an impostor. Said the prophet Isaiah, "To the law and to the testimony: if they speak not according to this word, it is because there is no light in them." Isaiah 8:20.

We can recognize an impostor by his words. No man, no angel who tells us anything contrary to God's Written Word is here on God's business!

We can also recognize an impostor by his works, by what he does. Jesus said, "By their fruits ye shall know them." Matthew 7:20.

God's angels don't go around playing tricks on people, scaring people, leading them on silly chases, making their telephones and TV sets and radios go berserk, making people lose their minds!

It is not difficult, of course, to spot an impostor when his words and works are consistently in open disagreement with the Bible. But fallen angels are too smart to lie all the time. We have to watch out for the subtle insinuations of doubt about the Scriptures, the slight misapplications of what the Scriptures say, the little bits of error mixed in with large quantities of truth. We have to beware of lies cloaked with deeds of mercy!

Satan is not stupid. His deceptions are more subtle, more clever, harder to identify than ever before. His fury increases with the shortness of his time. His power to deceive will escalate until God takes it away. Desperately ruthless, he will stop at nothing within the limits God has set. We are not safe for a moment except as we are kept by the power of God and His angels!

Reason enough for caution in our acceptance of the supernatural? Reason enough to watch for the telltale marks of the impostor—even in an angel of light? Reason enough to say, even to an angel, "Credentials, please"?

118

We live in an hour when the activities of fallen angels are being published far and wide. Spectacular? Yes. Undeniably supernatural. But often bizarre, full of bewitching fascination, deteriorating to mind and body and soul. Yet circulated everywhere and bought up by the unsuspecting, to their hurt!

It would be no surprise, then, if Satan should attempt to hinder the publishing of the activities of God's loyal angels. And he does not have to put presses out of commission in order to do this. What he cannot stop, he tries to discredit. And the sad fact is that sincere, well-meaning Christians have sometimes unwittingly played into his hands.

You see, there are sincere people with overactive imaginations. There are people who exaggerate without meaning to. There are good people who just don't have the ability to tell a story straight. There are people with faulty memories.

And then, unfortunately, there are those who simply won't let the facts get in the way of a good story. They have sacrificed their credibility on the altar of the dramatic and the spectacular. They have become good storytellers—so good that nobody believes them.

But does it have to be one or the other—a choice between a good story and the facts? Jesus was the Prince of storytellers. Yet He never compromised truth. He never let His hearers think that imagination was fact or that fact was imagination.

Satan would like to discredit every story of angel activity in this book if he could. And he doesn't have to attack the stories themselves. All he has to do is to question the credibility of those who have told them. It is unfortunate that a few have made it easy for him.

Some of my favorite stories have been left out of this book because a tendency to exaggerate, of which the tellers may have been quite unaware, has caused others to question the experiences they have told—experiences which may really have happened and which would have been a boost to the faith of many. (Please—many a story has been left out because of a lack of space, and uncounted experiences have not been included because I have never heard of them.)

It is to be hoped that no fiction or fantasy, no human exaggeration, has slipped into these pages—though the law of averages would tell us that is too much to hope. I think you can see that it would be impossible to check out the accuracy of so many experiences from which we are separated by time or space or both.

But I appeal to you, If you spot something you know to be inaccurate, a story that for some reason you personally can't believe, don't write off the rest. Satan would like to convince you that angel involvement in the lives of men and women today just doesn't happen, that it's all fiction. But it isn't, friend. It is very, very real. The stories in the Bible have been attacked too. Satan has tried to reduce them to the status of myth and legend. But they still stand.

Don't let the enemy push the ceiling of your faith down upon your head. Don't let him steal away the comfort and encouragement that can be yours as you realize that understanding, sympathizing, powerful angels are, in every time of need, not far away. Don't let anyone or anything rob you of the quiet, exhilarating sense of wonder as you contemplate what God is doing day by day with the assistance of powerful angels that never tire of the errands on which He sends them. Let the ceilings of your faith be pushed higher and higher until they are gone!

The day comes when we will see these patient, loving angels face-to-face. But we can know the wonder of their companionship even now!

In the Lions' Den Again

A mother said to her small son, "How was Sunday School?" And he replied, "Not good. Daniel's in the lions' den again."

And of course that is not good at all!

But is it possible that the experience of Daniel in the den of lions, and that of his three friends in the furnace, may shortly be repeated—with variations, of course, and with some of us as participants?

One cannot carefully read the books of Daniel and the Revelation without discovering a close tie between the two. And evidently Daniel, as well as Revelation, is a book written for the last days. Evidently religious oppression will soon raise its ugly head again. And the student of Daniel cannot escape the conviction that the experiences of Daniel and his friends, although they really happened, are in a sense a preview of things to come and are meant to be an encouragement to those of us who may find ourselves involved.

This brings up a question. Will men and women in the final days be called upon to give their lives for their Lord? Or has the day of martyrs passed? If the experience of Daniel and his friends is an encouragement for those who are delivered, what encouragement is there for those who are not?

We read that "there shall be a time of trouble, such as never was since there was a nation even to that same time: and at that time thy people shall be delivered, every one that shall be found written in the book." Daniel 12:1.

And we are told, "In the day of affliction, when the enemy presses us, we shall walk among the angels."[1]

Of the final days we read: "Though enemies may thrust them into prison, yet dungeon walls cannot cut off the communication between their souls and Christ. One who sees their every weakness, who is acquainted with every trial, is above all earthly powers; and angels will come to them in lonely cells, bringing light and peace from heaven. The prison will be as a palace; for the rich in faith dwell there, and the gloomy walls will be lighted up with heavenly light, as when Paul and Silas prayed and sang praises at midnight in the Philippian dungeon."[2]

In that day the ninety-first psalm will be literally fulfilled. "A thousand shall fall at thy side, and ten thousand at thy right hand; but it shall not come nigh thee. Only with thine eyes shalt thou behold and see the reward of the wicked."

"To human sight it will appear that the people of God must soon seal their testimony with their blood, as did the martyrs before them. They themselves begin to fear that the Lord has left them to fall by the hand of their enemies." But "could men see with heavenly vision, they would behold companies of angels that excel in strength stationed about those who have kept the word of Christ's patience. With sympathizing tenderness, angels have witnessed their distress, and have heard their prayers. They are waiting the word of their Commander to snatch them from their peril."[3]

"If the blood of Christ's faithful witnesses were shed at this time, it would not, like the blood of the martyrs, be as seed sown to yield a harvest for God. Their fidelity would not be a testimony to convince others of the truth; for the obdurate heart has beaten back the waves of mercy until they return no more. If the righteous were now left to fall a prey to their enemies, it would be a triumph for the prince of darkness. . . . Glorious will be the deliverance of those who have patiently waited for His coming, and whose names are written in the book of life."[4]

So there will be no martyrs at the very last. But what about the days *before* the very last, before the probation granted men has finally ended? May some of God's people yet be called upon to give up their lives for their Lord? Yes, they will. And will these be denied the comfort and strength of angel visits? Are angels sent only to those who are delivered from peril? Don't ever think it! Listen to this:

"They rejoiced that they were accounted worthy to suffer for the truth, and songs of triumph ascended from the midst of crackling flames. Looking upward by faith, they saw Christ and angels leaning over the battlements of heaven, gazing upon them with the deepest interest, and regarding their steadfastness with approval."[5]

And here is a statement that has long intrigued me: "Prayer has 'subdued kingdoms, wrought righteousness, obtained promises, stopped the mouths of lions, quenched the violence of fire'—we shall know what this means when we hear the reports of the martyrs who died for their faith."[6]

What will the martyrs tell us? Will they tell us that they felt no pain in the flames? Is that what this statement is suggesting?

It was an enemy who said of the martyrdom of Huss, and of Jerome, who died soon after: "Both bore themselves with constant mind when their last hour approached. They prepared for the fire as if they were going to a marriage feast. They uttered no cry of pain. When the flames rose, they began to sing hymns; and scarce could the vehemency of the fire stop their singing."[7]

Who gives a man such courage? God does. When it is needed. Not before.

A crisis is approaching—a crisis the like of which we have never seen. The decisions made in that crisis—to be true to our Lord or to betray Him—will be ours. The rest we can safely leave in His hands. We can say in quiet confidence, as did the three Hebrews: "If we are thrown into the blazing furnace, the God we serve is able to save us from it, and he will rescue us from your hand, O king. But even if he does not, we want you to know, O king, that we will not serve your gods or worship the image of gold you have set up." Daniel 3:17, 18, N.I.V.

Angels may be commissioned to deliver us. Or they may not be. Of one thing we can be certain. Our God is well able to duplicate any miracle of Daniel's day— even that of the blazing furnace. In fact, He has already demonstrated that ability—literally—in our day!

It is from Pastor John—whose real name I am not using—that we learn the thrilling story of a local pastor who was in charge of two of our districts in a country that I will not identify. There was fighting back and forth between the tribes, and it was a terrible situation. Pastor John had tried to get into the area to visit the local district pastor, for he knew that things were going rough. Once he got as far as the river that bordered the district—and he got that far only by traveling in the company of armed soldiers. But as they came up to the river, they saw that the bridge had been blown up in the tribal fighting and there was no way to get across. It was only a few weeks later that this amazing story came out.

This dedicated local pastor, with his wife and four children, was living in a little village. Many of his church members had fled into the jungle, for at that time the witch doctors had taken control of the area. And the witch doctors had decreed that anyone who refused to bow down to the native idols and sacrifice a chicken, anyone who retained any respect for a religion brought by a white man, anyone who dared to call himself a Christian must be killed. Orders had gone out that the people must revert to their old pagan worship with its ceremonies.

The pastor knew all this. It was because of this order that many of his people had taken refuge deep in the jungle and built little shelters there.

Once again he was advised to leave the village and join a little group of thirty-five or forty of his members in the jungle. But he still had seventy or eighty members in the village and felt he could not go.

Then one evening the report came that the witch doctors and their mobs were in a neighboring village four or five kilometers away. The pastor called his members together and told them to feel free to leave, but he felt that he must stay. They said, "Oh, but your house will be destroyed! Our church will be burned!"

They knew, and he knew, how easily those thatched-roof buildings would burn.

Later that evening two friends who were not Christians came and told him, "They are going to destroy the church and this house sometime tonight! Please, please leave! Flee into the jungle!"

He said he would pray about it and that if he felt impressed to leave he would leave. If not, he would remain.

He called his wife and four children together, and

they prayed. They prayed often that night. About midnight there was a hammering at the door and a vicious, barking order, "Open the door, or we will burn down your house!"

Again he gathered his little family, and there in the middle of the living room floor they quoted some of the Bible promises that meant so much to them.

The shouts increased outside. "Come out here! We'll give you one more chance—or we'll destroy you and your house!" But as he prayed, he felt he should remain where he was.

They heard the order outside, "Set it alight!" And soon they could hear the crackling of the dry thatched roof. Choking smoke and flames surrounded them. Then at the side window there was a hammering sound as the window was chopped open with axes. Two of the soldiers were standing there. They could see the pastor on his knees with his wife and children, praying. They sneered and threw one of the axes at the pastor, wounding his leg slightly. But he continued to pray. The roof was now totally ignited.

It was four weeks later that Pastor John was finally able to get into the area. He followed the little footpath eight miles out into the jungle, where a little Adventist village had been established. As he entered the little settlement, the pastor came running and threw his arms around him. Pastor John knew him well. They had grown up together. But he could hardly recognize him now as the neat, representatively dressed man he knew him to be. Here he was, in tattered clothes that he had not been able to replace because of the fighting. He was a pathetic figure. But as he threw his arms around his old friend, he told him the rest of the story.

He said, "That night, as my home was being burned, with the witch doctors and their fierce killers surrounding it, everything we had going up in smoke, we were praying. And as we prayed, we saw two figures much brighter than the flames come in that window. And they lifted us out of that room and brought us out here to the jungle!"

Ministering angels! And everything was all right!

But there was more. After the house had burned down, with only smoldering ashes and charred timbers left, the witch doctor ordered his men to bring out the bodies—the six bodies of that little family that had dared to defy his order. His men went in—the two who had stood at the window and seen them on their knees, who testified that they were right there in the middle of the room. But now there was only a smoldering mass of half-burned grass and jungle poles. They pulled the poles out and dug away the ashes. But they could find no bodies—no charred corpses to prove that they had been able to destroy this family that so defiantly trusted in an unseen God!

Three years after that experience one of the witch doctors became a humble follower of the Lord Jesus Christ because of what he had seen that night—the amazing manifestation of the love of God for His people and His power to deliver them by means of angels who excel in strength![8]

When No Angel Stays the Hand

Abraham had made his heart-wrenching surrender. He had raised the knife to take the life of his son—the son born of a miracle. And then—just at the critical moment, just in the nick of time—an angel stayed his hand!

But sometimes no angel stays the hand. Down through the centuries to this very moment, rising from this planet in an ever-increasing crescendo, is the persistent question "Why?"

Why, Lord? Why did You let Tommy die? Why didn't You stay the hand of death? Where were the angels when I needed them? Weren't You watching, Lord? Or were You busy somewhere else? I trusted. I believed. Why didn't You answer? Didn't You care? Why, Lord? Why?

Such is the language of broken hearts!

"Nothing shall by any means hurt you," said Jesus. But many have been hurt. "They shall lay hands on the sick, and they shall recover." But some have not recovered. "These signs shall follow them that believe." But many have believed—and seen no miracle at the critical hour. "On earth peace, good will toward men," said the angels. But the world's hurt is growing worse by the day. Where are the angels now? Why don't they stay the hand of trouble and violence and crime? Why doesn't God do something?

If only He could! If only we could understand how He longs to heal every hurt, to cool every fever, to mend every broken bone and broken heart, to set the world singing again. But He can't—yet!

If God should do for His trusting, believing people all that He longs to do—heal every one of them, keep the planes from crashing and the automobiles from colliding, prevent every accident, turn every bullet aside, permit no harm to come to one of His own—Satan would charge Him with giving His people an unfair advantage.

But it is more than that. If God should heal all the hurts, if He should stay the hand of violent death, if He should restrain the winds of the hurricane and turn aside the waters of every flood, if He should allow no plane to crash, if He should allow no catastrophe to take the lives of the innocent along with the guilty, men would never understand how cruel, how lethal, how ruthless sin is. And until men understand that, until it is burned indelibly into every mind in the universe, this reign of trouble can never be ended. God is in a hurry too. But He wants to do it right!

And so an angel stayed the hand of Abraham. An angel stopped the mouths of lions in Daniel's day. Jesus Himself walked in the blazing furnace with three men who refused to deny Him. Peter was delivered from prison. But John the Baptist died alone. And Paul. And no angel stayed the hand when the disciples of Jesus one by one—except John—died a violent death.

And no angel stayed the hand when Jesus endured the terrible ordeal that gave us the word Gethsemane. They were watching. They saw Him weighed down with the shuddering, mysterious dread. They saw the

129

fate of humanity trembling in the balance. They longed to go to His aid. But the decision to save man, or not to save him, must be His own. They saw the Father separating every beam of light from His Son—and knew then how offensive sin is to a holy God. They saw the cup tremble in His hand. They heard Him plead, "Father, if it be possible." But there was no escape for the Son of God. He must die. Or all humanity must die. Finally, His decision made, He fell dying to the ground!

And then, at that critical moment, the heavens opened. A brilliant light split the darkness as Gabriel, the mighty angel who took the place of Lucifer, came to the Saviour's side. Jesus' own special angel was sent—not to stay the hand, not to remove the cup, but to strengthen Him to drink it. He assured Him of His Father's love and told Him that a multitude of souls would be eternally saved by His sacrifice.

And then came Calvary. The mob was there. The executioners were there. The scoffers and the hypocrites were there. Satan was there—wringing the heart of Jesus with his fierce temptations. The fallen angels were there, casting their hellish shadow over the minds of men.

But God was there, too, in the shadows—near Him, loving Him, proud of Him—even as with breaking heart He removed the last evidence of His presence from His Son. And angels were there—watching in silence as they saw the Saviour crushed with the weight of all the sins of men, all the world's guilt at once. Watching in amazement as they saw how far Satan would go. Watching as the last trace of sympathy for the rebel leader was drained from their hearts. Watching as they saw Jesus defeating death and the author of death, making the universe forever safe from sin's deadly taint. Angels were there—their own hearts crushed and amazed by what they saw that day, by the awful depths of rebellion and the incredible heights of love enacted before them!

And then the Saviour cried, "It is finished."

In that final moment He knew that He had won. And angels knew. And Satan knew.

Is it any wonder that angels rejoiced that it was done?

Sometimes no angel stays the hand. But in God's incredible providence, out of the densest darkness shines the most brilliant light. For Jesus. For you. For me.

Swords of Straw

It happened in a country that I will not identify except to say that it is somewhere on this planet. And it happened to people who have never answered to the names used here. The important thing is that it happened!

The Terror. We might as well call him that. He was a bandit leader, a terrorist, and so ruthless a killer that the government had offered a huge reward for anyone who could bring him in dead or alive.

Attempts were made to subdue him. But he was out to destroy everything he didn't care for—and that included most everything and most everybody. This cunning bandit and his men were destroying everything in their path. The situation was desperate. Medicines were needed. Food was needed. But who could enter the danger zone?

Finally a contingent of the finest soldiers was sent in. But the Terror quickly disposed of them by simply setting a trap. He had his men dig a huge pit and then place spears and sharpened iron stakes in the bottom of it. It was so carefully camouflaged that the soldiers marched right into it—to their death.

Then one day Pastor John (mentioned in two earlier chapters) received a call from a government official, asking if he would try to take some medicines into that area.

Pastor John and his little group of workers prayed earnestly about this assignment, this challenge, from the government. And as they prayed, they remembered the promise, "For he shall give his angels charge over thee, to keep thee in all thy ways. They shall bear thee up in their hands, lest thou dash thy foot against a stone." Psalm 91:11, 12.

They felt that they must try.

And so the government provided three or four aircraft, which were then loaded with food, clothing, and medicines. These supplies—about a hundred tons in all—were flown as near as possible to the area controlled by the Terror. Then a convoy of seventeen trucks and two or three jeeps was sent, ready to take the supplies into the stricken territory.

As Pastor John left on his dangerous mission, the government official said to him, "Be careful. But God is with you." He told him to work closely with his commander in that section of the country.

But when Pastor John arrived, the colonel told him with a shake of his head, "It's impossible for you to go in." But then he said, "Wait. I have some soldiers that are on the fringes of that area, and at twelve o'clock each day they send me a report of the movements of the Terror."

It was on the fifth day that the report came in by radio that the Terror and his band had moved to another part of the country and that the main road into the area was now comparatively safe. They decided to try the next morning.

The convoy was loaded from the warehouses, and Pastor John was given a government driver that he had used before—a young man by the name of Peter. He was a good Christian and a careful driver. Though his loyalty was to the government, he happened to be a member of the Terror's tribe, and so he knew the language. Pastor John, incidentally, had learned the Terror's tribal language too, as a young man, for he had worked in that area.

They started out that morning, Pastor John and Peter in the lead jeep. The colonel had told them that the first part of their journey would be the most dangerous. It was through a valley. And as they drove through that valley, the pastor kept thinking of David's words, "the valley of the shadow of death." For it was just that. In the road were corpses that the Terror's men had left. Along the sides of the road were stakes, with women impaled on the stakes, gashed open—hideous scenes that one never expects to see in a lifetime.

Then as they proceeded farther into the Terror's territory, the roads were so filled with dead bodies that they stopped. They tried to pull some of the bodies aside, but they could not, for it would delay them in reaching a point of safety that evening. So they just had to put those vehicles in four-wheel drive and grind over the corpses as they proceeded.

They got out of that valley. The colonel had told them that when they climbed the escarpment they would be out of the danger zone. And what a prayer of thanksgiving they offered when they reached the top!

They knew it would take the heavily loaded trucks about half an hour to get up that very difficult grade. So Peter and the pastor decided to go on and wait for them at a village a little way ahead.

They started on with lighter hearts. They could make better time now. It was a high, level, flat plateau with clumps of dense jungle through which they had to pass.

They were going through one of those dense clumps

134

of jungle when suddenly Peter jerked the wheel to the left and they piled into the ditch, the jeep on its side. There they were, hugging each other tightly, and the pastor said, "What's your trouble? What happened?"

And Peter said, "Oh, we're going to die! They're going to kill us!"

"What's the matter?"

"Oh, I've seen the Terror's sign of an ambush! I've seen his sign!"

Only to his own tribesmen would the Terror give the warning. The secret sign was in a conspicuous place so that members of his own tribe would know that ahead was a trap.

Two minutes passed. Three, four, maybe five minutes passed. Nothing happened. The pastor tried to climb out of the jeep, but Peter pulled him back on top of him again. "No! You must not get out!"

Finally, with great difficulty, Pastor John did climb out. He stood at the edge of the road and looked around. He could see nothing suspicious—except that there were fresh tracks in the road. And he had the strange feeling that he was being watched.

He was impressed by the Spirit of God to say something. So he put his little portable transistorized loud speaker to his mouth and spoke in the language of the tribe through whose territory they were passing. He just said to the trees and the jungle around him, "We have come as friends. I am pastor of the Seventh-day Adventist Church. I am here to help you. Anybody in this area who needs help, we are here to help you. We are not here as enemies but as friends."

Nothing happened. Everything was quiet. It was deathly still!

Then out of the silence came the snap of two dry twigs. Snap! Snap! It was a signal—a signal that he had learned as a boy. It was a challenging signal, and a reply must be given. Someone off in the jungle was challenging their passage. If he could come up with the right word, everything would be all right. But it had been twelve or fourteen years since he had used that word—that password—and he had forgotten it.

He flashed a message on the frequency of heaven. And like another flash, that word came back to the tip of his tongue. He shouted it out. It was the right word!

Again he said through his loudspeaker, "Friend, whoever you are out there, please come and let's shake hands." And he gave in the tribal language the respectful greeting that only the big chiefs receive. Again nothing happened.

Then, off to the right, there was a rustle in the jungle. The leaves moved, and onto the edge of the road stepped a tall, handsome, fine-looking warrior with an automatic rifle in his hand, pointed right at him.

The pastor said, "Friend, put down your gun, please. I have no weapons. I'm here as a friend."

The warrior took two or three more steps toward him, with that automatic rifle still pointed right at him. He could see that he was some tremendous leader. Again he gave the respectful greeting.

Finally he laid down his gun and approached cautiously, suspiciously. As he approached, the pastor extended his hand. The warrior looked at him, clasped his hand, and said in surprise, "Pastor John, what are you doing here?"

He had war paint on his forehead and decorating his cheeks. The pastor couldn't recognize him, and so he said, "Do you know me?"

"Yes, yes, of course I know you. Don't you know me?"

"Who are you?"

"I am the Terror."

The pastor was holding a huge reward in his hand,

as it were. And this terribly feared bandit knew him!

"Don't you remember? I am Henry from the village of Wait. You used to teach us in your little Branch Sabbath School, thirteen or fifteen years ago. I am Henry. Don't you remember me, Pastor John?"

Of course he remembered him! And the boy Henry was now this feared bandit!

As the pastor held his hand, the Terror began to tremble like a leaf in the wind. His whole body was shaking. He said, "Now I understand. Now I understand. For the first time in my life my voice disappeared. My voice was taken from me. I tried to give an order as your jeep went into the ditch—an order for my men to kill. But I couldn't find a voice. My voice was taken away. And as I looked at the wheels spinning around on your jeep, I could see soldiers standing around, heavily armed. I could see these soldiers off in the road behind you. They didn't look like any soldiers I have ever seen."

He went on. "Now I understand. Those stories you used to tell us, those picture rolls you used to show us—of your God, of those angels that your God sends." He was still trembling. "Now I understand. Those beings that looked like the moon and like the stars were angels from your God! Oh, Pastor John, what are you doing here?"

What a thrill! He told him what he was doing there. And he knew that those mighty angels from heaven were still standing right there beside them. For this terrible killer, this man skilled in destruction and death, was still trembling!

They talked for two or three minutes, and then the Terror heard the trucks approaching. He said, "Pastor John, are there soldiers in those trucks?"

"Yes, Henry, but they are under my control. They are under my orders."

"Oh, but they will kill me!"

He had heard. He knew that there was a tremendous price on his head. But the pastor assured him, "There will be no killing here today. God and His angels are here. There will be no killing today!"

The trucks were still some distance away, and the pastor said to him, "Friend, you have seen today a wonderful demonstration of God's love for you. I did not see those soldiers, those angels that you saw. But I know that just one of those angels could have annihilated you and your men. But God loves you. That same Jesus that you heard about under the trees in the village of Wait, fifteen years ago, is still speaking to you. Promise me, friend—promise me, Henry—that you will give up this life of destruction, that you will respect and honor the love of the Jesus who has saved your life, who wants to give you eternal life with Him!"

Still trembling, he hesitated and looked around. The pastor asked how many men he had with him in the jungle and asked him to call them. He gave an order, and dozens of heavily armed bandits came out from both sides of that jungle. They couldn't understand what had happened to their proud and haughty leader who grasped the hand of a white man, a member of the race they were sworn to destroy. They looked at him with cruelty and death in their eyes.

As his men approached, the Terror said to them, "This man's skin is white, but his heart is the same as ours. He is our friend."

They gathered around him, and he told them about his voice disappearing, about the soldiers from heaven, and that the pastor had assured him they were still standing there, watching over their meeting.

Then the pastor asked him again, "Will you promise to give up this terrible life of destruction and slaughter?"

And there in the presence of his men—he promised!

It took a long time to persuade the government that the Terror was a converted man. Top officials were convinced only when they saw that the horrible reign of terror had completely subsided. Then another proclamation was issued, explaining briefly that the Terror was now a Christian and that the price on his head was no longer an offer. The radio blared the news. The newspapers carried it in headlines.

And Pastor John kept remembering the words of his father, spoken to him as a frightened boy of ten, "Sonny, our Father in heaven has sent His angels to be with us. Everything will be all right."[1]

What a story! It lifts us right into the presence of the celestial beings that see the face of God!

I see in that story a reminder of how angels, down through the centuries, have stayed the hands lifted against God's trusting children. Men struck dumb. Arms paralyzed. Swords broken. Pistols that have jammed or misfired. All the times when angel hands have come between God's people and their enemies.

But there is more. I see in that story a preview of the days ahead—when the ministry of angels will become more real to us than ever before. Listen to these words from the servant of the Lord:

"It is impossible to give any idea of the experience of the people of God who shall be alive upon the earth when celestial glory and a repetition of the persecution of the past are blended. They will walk in the light proceeding from the throne of God. By means of the angels there will be constant communication between heaven and earth."[2]

Impossible to describe it, to comprehend what it will be. But let your imagination hold it before the mind's eye. Hardship? Yes. Persecution? Yes. Tears?

139

Yes. But angels coming and going. Constant communication with heaven. Celestial glory here on earth. Angels leading some to mountain retreats. Prisons like a palace. The caves of earth a rendezvous with angels. God's lamps all lighted. The sky from here to Orion ablaze with the lights of home!

And I see in the story of the Terror a preview of the day of broken swords: "The heavenly sentinels, faithful to their trust, continue their watch. . . . Enemies will in some cases . . . endeavor to take their [commandment keepers'] lives. But none can pass the mighty guardians stationed about every faithful soul. Some are assailed in their flight from the cities and villages; but the swords raised against them break and fall as powerless as a straw. Others are defended by angels in the form of men of war."[3]

That's what the story of the Terror means to me!

But why the ministry of angels? Is it only that we may be entertained—and momentarily awed—by glimpses of their brightness and stories of their power? Is it just to keep us comfortable in the knowledge of their protection while we go on adding years to our stay on this planet? Is it only to keep us content and safe—on this side of Jordan?

No, friend. The morning will not always wait. No matter how content we are with things of earth, "the end will come more quickly than men expect."[4]

In the meantime, the little bit of meantime that is left, the winds of temptation will be fierce, our faith will be battered but not broken in the gale, the storm of opposition will threaten to overwhelm us.

But God will still be on the throne. And He will send His angels. And everything will be all right!

NOTES

It Must Have Been an Angel

1. Told by Tay Thomas in *Guideposts* (April 1965) and quoted by Catherine Marshall in *Something More*.
2. *Education*, p. 304.

Now You See Them

1. Told by Ruth Wheeler in *Light the Paper Lantern*, pp. 15-19.
2. *The Acts of the Apostles*, p. 154.
3. *Education*, pp. 304, 305.
4. Braith Brandt, as told to LaVern Tucker in *Quiet Hour Echoes*, May 1978.
5. Deborah S. Spicer in *Insight*, January 20, 1976.
6. Isaac Neabaugo in *Insight*, February 5, 1974.
7. *The Ministry of Healing*, p. 417.

Now You Don't

1. Hazel A. Jackson in *Review and Herald*, March 25, 1976.
2. Related to the author by Ruth Grunke.
3. *Education*, p. 271.
4. *Ibid.*, p. 305.
5. Raymond Woolsey, *Joy in the Morning*, p. 182.

Guards in White

1. Related to the author by Garth Thompson.
2. *The Hand That Intervenes*, pp. 23, 24.
3. Related by Angie Bancarz to Paul Ricchiuti.

In Time of Peril

1. *The Hand That Intervenes*, pp. 21, 22.
2. *Ibid.*, pp. 190-192.

Sometimes a Dream

   1. Len H. Barnard in *Review and Herald*, August 26, 1971.
   2. Jane Allen in *Review and Herald*, October 20, 1977.
   3. Bobbie Rix in *Adventist Review*, May 18, 1978.
   4. Related to the author by Arla Munson.

Sometimes a Voice

   1. Related to the author by Pastor Leonard Robinson, who is Pastor John in the story.
   2. Catherine Marshall in *A Man Called Peter*, pp. 14, 15.
   3. Related to the author by Pastor Lloyd Wyman.
   4. Related to the author by Jack Circle.
   5. Letter 144—1902. Used by permission of the Ellen G. White Estate.
   6. Ellen G. White in *Review and Herald*, November 22, 1898. Emphasis supplied.
   7. *The Great Controversy*, p. 632.
   8. Related to the author by Pastor Alger Johns.

Stand-ins

   1. *The Ministry of Healing*, p. 481.
   2. *The Hand That Intervenes*, pp. 143, 144.
   3. *Ibid.*, pp. 144, 145.
   4. *Ibid.*, p. 146.
   5. Told by Bob Sherman in a Pacific Press worship.
   6. Esther L. Vogt in *Ministry*, March 1978, reprinted from *Guideposts*, July 1977.
   7. George A. Buttrick in *Jesus Came Preaching*, pp. 38, 39.

Replay

   1. *Christ's Object Lessons*, p. 149.
   2. *Testimonies*, vol. 8, p. 12.
   3. *The Desire of Ages*, p. 336.
   4. *Testimonies*, vol. 8, p. 10.
   5. *The Desire of Ages*, p. 664.
   6. *The Hand That Intervenes*, pp. 93, 94.
   7. *Ibid.*, pp. 98-100.
   8. Paul B. Ricchiuti in *Adventist Review*, January 5, 1978.
   9. Irma Kaplan in *Review and Herald*, November 27, 1975.
   10. Jeanette A. Snorrason in *Review and Herald*, July 12, 1973.
   11. Einar Thuesen in *Review and Herald*, January 30, 1975.
   12. Hector V. Gayares in *Review and Herald*, November 3, 1977.
   13. Related to the author by Alice Kuhn.
   14. Told by Duane Tank in a Pacific Press worship.

Out On a Limb

1. *The Hand That Intervenes*, pp. 172, 173.
2. *Ibid.*, pp. 211-213.
3. *Patriarchs and Prophets*, p. 290.
4. *The Desire of Ages*, p. 125.
5. *Selected Messages*, bk. 1, p. 282.
6. *Liberty News*, October 1969, reprinted from *Underground Evangelism*, September 1969.
7. 1978 Vacation Bible School Program Helps.

The Touch of Angel Hands

1. Frances Daisy Duffie, as told to Martha Duffie, in the *Youth's Instructor*, April 20, 1965.
2. *The Desire of Ages*, p. 143.
3. Ritchie Way in *Adventist Review*, February 23, 1978.

They Also Care

1. Related to the author by Ruth Elliott.
2. *The Acts of The Apostles*, p. 561.
3. *Early Writings*, p. 39.
4. *My Life Today*, p. 307.
5. *The Desire of Ages*, p. 21.
6. Ellen G. White in *Review and Herald*, November 22, 1898.
7. *Early Writings*, p. 127.
8. As told by Mrs. Louise Dubay to C. F. O'Dell, in *Review and Herald*, December 22, 1955.
9. *Education*, p. 305.

Touching the Fringes

1. Barbara Huff in *Adventist Review*, March 29, 1979.
2. Related to the author by Ruth Gibson.
3. *Pacific Union Recorder*, February 16, 1953.
4. Related to the author by Jack Circle.
5. B. J., as told to Maria Anne Hirschmann, in *Insight*, August 24, 1971.
6. Related to the author by Kay Buzelli.
7. David H. Sharpe in *Review and Herald*, December 15, 1977.
8. Janine Saunders, a pseudonym, in *Insight*, May 30, 1978.
9. V. F. Smith in *Signs of the Times*, January 1976.

The Wonder of Commitment

1. *The Desire of Ages*, p. 200.
2. Virgil Robinson in *Adventist Review*, January 12, 1978.
3. *The Desire of Ages*, p. 668.
4. *Drumbeat of Love*, p. 186.

The Clock That Struck Thirteen
  1. *The Hand That Intervenes*, pp. 188, 189.

The Bushman's Story
  1. Gladys Piatt Ansley in the *Youth's Instructor*, January 22, 1963.

Only One Key
  1. Cyril J. Davey, *The Story of Sadhu Sundar Singh*, pp. 31-34, 89-92, 108-110.

The Thunder at Eight
  1. From a Peter Marshall sermon included in *A Man Called Peter*, by Catherine Marshall, pp. 117-119.

Credentials, Please
  1. As related to the author by June Keyt.

In the Lions' Den Again
  1. *Maranatha*, p. 95.
  2. *The Great Controversy*, p. 627.
  3. *Ibid.*, p. 630.
  4. *Ibid.*, p. 634.
  5. *Ibid.*, p. 41.
  6. *Christ's Object Lessons*, p. 172.
  7. Quoted in *The Great Controversy*, p. 110.
  8. Related to the author by Pastor Leonard Robinson, who is Pastor John in the story.

Swords of Straw
  1. Related to the author by Pastor Leonard Robinson, who is Pastor John in the story.
  2. *Testimonies*, vol. 9, p. 16.
  3. *The Great Controversy*, p. 631.
  4. *Ibid.*, p. 631.